Refuge

By
Geshe Dakpa Topgyal

Author's Dedication

Through the force of the Merit created from writing this book,
May His Holiness the Dalai Lama enjoy good health and live long.
May his work for world peace be highly effective and bear great success,
And may sustainable peace and harmony prevail in every corner of the world.

May the Dharma last long.
May the Dharma holder live long.
May the hearts and minds of all beings be filled with love and compassion, and
May the love and compassion be the effective tool for bringing peace and happiness in the world.

In all rebirths: myself and others,
May we never be apart from the Three Jewels.
May we always be protected and guided by the Triple Gem.
And may their blessings enter into us in all time and space.

Whoever reads this book,
May they find deep spiritual joy.
May their mind and heart be awakened
To love, compassion and morality.

Refuge

Acknowledgement

This book would not have been possible without the help of my devoted student Sheila Low-Beer. I owe her many thanks for her generous help and tireless work in correcting my messy manuscript and editing it in a proper order.

Giving birth to this book was painful but indeed worthwhile if it is beneficial.

Homage

Kyab Ney Kon Chok Sum La Na Mo!
 I bow and Prostrate to the Three Jewels, the ultimate object of Refuge.

Contents

Author's Introduction			ix
CHAPTER ONE		Dharma, Refuge and Karma	1
CHAPTER TWO		The Meaning of Refuge	7
CHAPTER THREE		The Six Realms of Samsara	13
CHAPTER FOUR		The Objects to Which You Go for Refuge	23
CHAPTER FIVE		The Objects to Which You Go for Refuge: Buddha	35
CHAPTER SIX		The Objects to Which You Go For Refuge: Dharma and Sangha	43
CHAPTER SEVEN		The Proper Way You Go for Refuge	47
CHAPTER EIGHT		Refuge Precepts to be Observed	53
CHAPTER NINE		Karma	59
CHAPTER TEN		The Negative Actions to be Avoided	63
CHAPTER ELEVEN		The Positive Deeds to be Cultivated	75
CHAPTER TWELVE		To Become a Buddhist Through Taking the Refuge Ordination	87
Appendix		Food Blessing and Prostration Prayer	93
About the Author			97

Author's Introduction

I traveled to many of the European countries, and particularly in one hundred and twenty cities of the United States of America during 1993 and 1994. The main purpose of my travel was to introduce Tibetan Buddhism to the Western world with an intention to awaken people's minds to 1. the true purpose of human life and 2. the idea of love, compassion, and morality as the inner goal and the means to attain peace, happiness, and universal harmony.

The purpose of Buddhist teaching is surely not to convert anyone to Buddhism but rather is to produce a good human being on this earth. However, as a result of hearing teachings in the West, many people have chosen to become practicing Buddhists instead of remaining within their previous religion and integrating Buddhist concepts into their religious practice.

Approximately seventeen million American people now claim to be Buddhists. However, I have found that many of those whom I have met do not have full understanding of Refuge. Refuge is the most essential factor for one to be a true Buddhist regardless of whether one has formally taken Refuge or not.

Of course, formally taking Refuge is extremely important, but having a full understanding of Refuge is the primary prerequisite for taking Refuge. It is important for oneself to fully understand Refuge and not to be a dry or an artificial Buddhist.

It is my intention that this book on Refuge will make sure people understand what "Refuge" really is—before making the important decision to take Refuge as a formal way to become a Buddhist.

Though most of the books on Buddhism touch on the subject of Refuge, they do not do so exclusively or in a broader way. In this book one will find a more dense and elaborated discussion on Refuge which will surely help you to understand what Refuge really is, and the whole purpose of taking Refuge.

Formally taking Refuge based on the correct understanding of Refuge is the healthiest way to become a Buddhist and the only way to become a true Buddhist. Through taking Rufuge one will become an irreversible student of the Buddha, a true learner. You will become fully content, comfortable and confident in the path practice, having no room in yourself to see others' beliefs as a threat, and you will observe the natural laws of karma as part of everyday life.

May this book be highly beneficial to all who read it.

Many prayers,
Geshe Dakpa Topgyal

Refuge *is the sacred entrance to the **Dharma**, and the Dharma is the peaceful path that consists of love, compassion, ethics, meditation and wisdom, with a strict root principle of non-violent conduct required on the part of the practitioner.*

CHAPTER ONE

Dharma, Refuge and Karma

The **Dharma**—the Buddhist teachings and training on the path to enlightenment—are based on the strong foundation of the principles of *Ahimsa* and *Drsti*. *Ahimsa* and *Drsti* are words in Sanskrit, the ancient language in which Lord Buddha gave all of his Mahayana teachings 2600 years ago for the enduring benefit of mankind.

Ahimsa means non-violence or non-harming conduct. By embracing *ahimsa* one makes a strong and firm commitment not to do harm to any living being whatsoever and to provide help to others in all times and circumstances as much as you can. *Drsti* means view, the view of the interdependent nature of reality—nothing is the creation of supernatural force, nor is it a random causeless manifestation. Rather, all animate and inanimate things are mere productions of causes and conditions, manifesting the force of the natural interdependent relationship among all things that exist—including you yourself.

In taking **Refuge** you are brought deep into the Dharma with an understanding of the complex working of the karmic causes and effects, to which all beings are subject. The combination of Refuge and a strong trust in the karmic causes and effects will generate an irreversible commitment to observe and not neglect or disregard the natural law of karma. This commitment will fulfill your aspiration to be happy in this life as well as to secure the happiness of your future rebirth.

Because you observe the law of **karma** you will surely experience much less conflict, disharmony, and mental, emotional, and psychological pain and sufferings, and there will be more room for joy, harmony, and mental peace and clarity.

In your next rebirth you will certainly find a fortunate and happy life in a realm conducive to your practice. You will experience joy, harmony, strong health, abundance of material wealth, attractive physical appearance, kind and gentle mind, reliable friends and loved ones, great success, strong mind and good heart; you will not be subject to external negative forces, and you will meet with a wholesome teacher—the source of virtue, wisdom, knowledge, and ethics.

Refuge assists your Dharma practice to become more effective, with a smooth progress free of hindrances caused by the evil tempters or Mara. (In Buddhism the evil tempters or Mara refer to those subtle tendencies within ourselves that cause us to act unvirtuously and that induce many illusions.) Observing the law of karma is the root of joy, happiness and harmony and causes all excellent good qualities of heart and mind to arise. Refuge will help you to gather all the necessary right growing conditions for your spiritual progress.

Why do I need to go for Refuge?

You need to go for Refuge in order to seek the mental and spiritual cause for joy and happiness. In your present condition you are always subject to pain and sufferings beyond your control. The physical world in which you live today, and you yourself, are of the nature of pain and suffering. Both the external world and your own life and body are subject to change, decay, age, sickness, death, and many mental and psychological distresses and diseases. Fear, stress, depression, sadness, loneliness, anxiety, and confusion are fundamental and persistent components of human neurosis. Many people, perhaps yourself, need psychiatric help and rely on Prozac and other abusive drugs to elevate mood. These are the clear proof that your life and the world in which you live are of the nature of suffering no matter how much you try to deny Buddha's teaching that "life is suffering."

Life is suffering

Your life may have begun by bringing joy and celebration on the earth, but, beyond your control, life ends in sadness, grief, and a tearful funeral service. This is also the proof of life as suffering. Life contains the inherent seed or malaise for the sprout of pain throughout.

Every day on global news you hear about such and such millionaires, Hollywood movie stars, famous writers, artists, singers, dancers, highly educated doctors, lawyers, professors and great world leaders. Many of these are habitually relying on sleeping pills to induce an artificial sleep because they do not have healthy natural sleep due to the stress, anxiety, and worry that dominate their mind. This is also the clear proof that ordinary life is suffering no matter what you have—name, wealth, high social status, power, or an important high-paying professional job which makes your life outstanding in the world.

Also, you hear in the news that such and such millionaire or famous star has committed suicide, or has been admitted in the psychiatric hospital. All of these are the clear and explicit proof that life is suffering and no external thing can bring you fully satisfying joy and happiness. External material things can surely bring you a momentary pleasure but soon that pleasure turns into the unexpected pain of dissatisfaction, frustration, confusion, and a painful need of more to get relief after relief.

You are constantly in need of something new, different, and more to feel good and find relief. This is how you live every day, but what is surprising is that you still do not recognize this as suffering and pain.

You need to solve this problem of suffering but you do not know how to solve it owing to the lack of a guide who can show you the way to do it. That is why you need to seek Refuge: in order to find the method to solve the problem and attain true irreversible happiness.

You not only experience samsaric pain and suffering in this life but in the next rebirth too. There is the high risk that you may experience a more intense form of pain in your next life if you disregard the natural law of karma and neglect to cultivate virtue and merit while as a human you have the **free will** and all opportunity.

To avoid suffering

The only way to avoid intense suffering in the next rebirth is to make effort to observe the law of karma and to rely on the Buddha, Dharma, and Sangha with trust and faith in their unfailing capability to help you to succeed in this through practicing the ethical conduct of cultivating wholesome deeds and discarding negative ones through every means and effort.

A proper practice of ethics based on the firm commitment of **Refuge** will make you successful in securing the joy and happiness of your next life while making your present life meaningful and wholesome. Unless you take Refuge no ethical conduct can serve as the ground or foundation for the higher spiritual cause for joy and happiness. **In the Buddhist tradition, true Dharma practice is not possible in the absence of Refuge.**

The Dharma is the one that brings inner transformation through which the real possibility for attaining long lasting joy and happiness and overcoming pain and suffering can surely occur. For this to happen is solely dependent on taking Refuge in your heart by realizing the **Buddha** as the supreme teacher of the truth, the **Dharma** as the unfailing tool or path, and the **Sangha** as an amazing strong support for the inner strength that you need to walk on the path and not be discouraged due to the long and painful journey to enlightenment.

If you are seeking the true happiness of liberation, you must go for Refuge as a ground foundation for the entire path practice to complete your spiritual goal. In general there are three levels of spiritual goal:

1. To obtain higher fortunate rebirth and secure future happiness
2. To attain full freedom from samsaric pain and sufferings so that you would not be ever subject to karma and delusion with their underlying subtle root of ignorance
3. To attain full enlightenment for the sake of all living beings with an altruistic concern for their well-being and a strong wish to lead them to enlightenment.

Acharya Chandrakirti in his *Seventy Verses On Refuge* said:

> *Whoever seeks liberation must go for Refuge. . . .*
> *The Buddha, Dharma, and Sangha*
> *Are the refuge for those who seek liberation.*

The Buddha, Dharma, and Sangha are three necessary factors in the process of getting free from samsaric pain and sufferings. **Buddha** is like a healer who first diagnoses precisely the nature of illness with its root cause. **Dharma** is like a panacea medicine which heals the illness from its cause, not just by treating the symptoms. **Sangha** is like an experienced and compassionate nurse who sincerely cares for and looks after the ill person by providing all comfort, courage, and hope. All of these contribute to the process of healing and recovery.

A true liberation seeker needs all three—Buddha, Dharma and Sangha—to walk on the path in order to cure all forms of samsaric pain and sufferings from their root cause. Without all three you will not be able to complete the path and accomplish the goal. On the other hand, you do not need anything more than these three since they offer a fully complete guide to enlightenment. Therefore, the Buddha, Dharma, and Sangha are said to be the **three rare Jewels.**

The liberation seeker or true Dharma practitioner must begin the path practice that primarily consists of love, compassion, ethics, meditation, and

wisdom by openly and sincerely going for Refuge in the Three Jewels. In order to go for Refuge you must recognize the Buddha as a flawless teacher of the supreme truth who does not have the potential to lie or deceive, and who does not have room to be mistaken with regard to the fact of reality. Then the Dharma, Buddha's teaching, can be found to be the true and unfailing path to enlightenment. Then the Sangha, those who live according to the teachings, who practice sincerely to gain some admirable good qualities, and who resonate their inner qualities through their actions and deeds are also found to be objects of trust and reverence.

Going for Refuge in the Three Jewels through seeing them with these excellent qualities will surely inspire you with a strong wish and interest to abide in the teachings of Dharma and practice it with your best effort and capability. Due to the Refuge your Dharma practice will be very effective with a smooth progress. Your delusions will become less strong, less prevalent; they will dominate your mind less, and they will dictate your actions and deeds less and less. Because of this you will experience more joy, peace, calmness, and harmony with your surroundings. Gradually you will gain higher realization. All of this will happen due to the sacredness of the Refuge.

It is important to point out that Refuge is the gateway to virtue, merit, and confident realization of the subtle working mechanisms of the natural law of karma. In Buddhism, without having Refuge in your heart nothing can have a positive meaning or power regardless of what practices you do—such as recitation of prayers and mantras, prostrations, making offerings, reading sutras, and performing ceremonies, etc.

When the Refuge is absent from your heart, your practice is like a seed that has been burnt. The Sutra says:

In those who lack refuge
Nothing positive will grow,
Just as from a burnt seed
No shoots will ever sprout.

Refuge—the most precious of all your inner resources

Refuge is the most precious of all your inner resources, an inexhaustible fund of virtue and merit. It carries you along the path to enlightenment like a pair of strong legs, and assembles every positive thing for you like a pair of strong arms.

When you begin your daily practice with taking Refuge and recollecting the good qualities of the Three Jewels, then your Dharma practice will be empowered with their blessings, grace, and uplifting energy. In Buddhism, that is why the Refuge is essential: it functions as a foundation stone for every spiritual development.

To take Refuge in the Three Jewels with an altruistic intention to benefit all living beings by leading them to attain enlightenment is the way of Mahayana refuge, and it is the entrance to infinite merit and virtue.

CHAPTER TWO

The Meaning of Refuge

Refuge is not a form of worship. It is all about the proper ways to place your trust in the Three Jewels with a serious intention to live according to the wholesome teachings to help yourself to attain liberation or enlightenment. Liberation or enlightenment certainly does not come to you as a gift from Buddha that is delivered to your door by overnight Fedex.

When you take Refuge you are not seeing Buddha's enlightened qualities as unattainable by anyone except the Buddha. Similarly you are not asking Buddha to give you something; you are not putting everything into the Buddha's hands to save you through seeing him as the ultimate savior. This is not what meant by taking Refuge in the Three Jewels in Buddhism.

In Buddhism, instead, the Buddha, Dharma and Sangha are the true source of blessing and inspiration, the field for accumulating merit, and your assistant in the process of creating conducive conditions and averting negative forces that could hinder you during your long journey to enlightenment.

The four critical factors

The complete meaning of Refuge can be conveyed through four critical factors. The great Kadampa masters of the past (even before the time of Jey Lama Tsongkhapa Chenpo, who founded the Geluk tradition of Tibetan Buddhism in the late 13th and early 14th century) used this unique way to explain Refuge.

The four main or critical factors through which the whole meaning of Refuge can be explained are:

1. The inner causes of going for Refuge
2. The objects to whom you should go for Refuge
3. The proper mode and manner of going for Refuge
4. The stages of the precepts you must abide by once you have taken Refuge

The inner causes of going for Refuge

In general there are many causes of going for Refuge. Among the various causes there are two which are mandatory and indispensable for taking Refuge in the Three Jewels. The two main causes are: 1. **fear** of samsaric pain and sufferings and 2. **lucid faith** in the capability of the Three Jewels to guide you on the path to freedom from all types of samsaric pain and sufferings through the wholesome teachings.

First I will discuss at length the **grounds for fear** of samsaric pain and sufferings. This fear has three levels:

1. Fear of personal concern that you risk falling into lower rebirth in the miserable realm in your next life
2. Fear of concern about general samsaric pain and suffering that pervade all forms of life in all three realms of existence no matter where you take rebirth
3. Fear of concern that all living beings are subject to pain and sufferings—beings who are like your own mother or who have once been your mother in one of your earlier lives through beginningless time.

These three types of fear are based on a legitimate factual reason. Just as going for Refuge is the gateway to Dharma and its practices, the gateway for taking Refuge is **fear**. As the first step in going for Refuge, therefore, it is essential to develop a fear of the sufferings of samsara in general, and particularly a fear of the sufferings of unfortunate lower rebirth in the miserable realms.

In order to develop such fear that pierces your heart, you must know what is samsara and what are the various types of pain and sufferings stemming from karma and delusions for which modern science has no solution. The basic human problem remains the same though science and technology are highly advanced and seem to have reached the peak in today's world.

The sufferings of samsara

Samsara in Sanskrit means a vicious cycle of birth and death characterized by seen and unseen pain and sufferings that cannot be avoided by any ordinary means but only through the practice of Dharma. This vicious cycle is put in motion by the wind force of karma and delusions that stands behind each individual living being. Unless you destroy the karma and delusion there is no way to stop the cycle and therefore basic human pain and suffering remain unsolved regardless of how much we put effort to improve the quality of science and its method.

In samsara the meaning of suffering goes much further and much deeper than the sufferings of war, hunger, poverty, and other physical and mental distresses or unpleasant sensations. Samsaric sufferings are like a deep and vast fire field covered with a thin layer of ashes. Because with your naive mind you don't see the fire field under the layer of ash, you constantly fall into the fire field and get severely burnt; this causes you to suffer for a long time with no relief at all.

The severely-burnt-like samsaric suffering has three levels in terms of their subtleties and severity. They are : **suffering of suffering, suffering of change, and suffering of pervasive conditioning or all-pervasive suffering**. You might be able to escape from the suffering of war, poverty, hunger, and minor unpleasant sensations but you cannot escape from these three levels of samsaric suffering regardless of how powerful, smart and cunning you are.

The first type of suffering—**suffering of suffering**—includes all evident unwanted feelings and sensations associated with your body and mind. For instance: sickness that turns your body into a skeleton and makes you weak like a very wilted flower petal; aging that distorts your appearance and makes you look unattractive; death that forces you to leave this world and sends you into the next without a guide or a light to see in the darkness of your own fear and confusion.

Even in the short periods when you are not having these experiences, still you suffer from displeasure, discomfort, confusion, fear, stress, anxiety, loneliness, sadness, separation from loved ones, not getting what you desire, getting what you don't want, dissatisfaction with what you have, always wanting more, different and new. After going through all these unpleasantnesses you face death and all this concludes with a tearful funeral service. A piece of stone carved with your name remains in the bare lonely cemetery. Thus ends one painful chapter of your endless life in the cycle of samsara, and a new chapter of life will begin with the same content of pain and sufferings. Samsara is a painful vicious cycle that has almost no end.

The second level of suffering—**suffering of change**—refers to all of your momentary pleasures to which you are prone to attach. All of your sensual pleasures are not only momentary but each one contains a seed for unexpected pain and sufferings. It is also correct to say that indulgence in the momentary pleasures always causes new pain and sufferings. It is like licking honey on a razor blade. The moment you experience the sweet taste of the honey you already begin to suffer from cutting your tongue. Every momentary pleasure is in the nature of pain as revealed through its change. Therefore, the second level of suffering is named the suffering of change.

Having no desire or clinging attachment to momentary pleasures is far better than having the desire to indulge and experience endless pleasure. You should realize that momentary pleasure never helps to bring full satisfaction and happiness. The more you indulge the more you want. This deepens your problems of dissatisfaction that have no remedy except that you cut the string of clinging attachment to pleasure.

The sensory pleasures are like a momentary relief or pleasure arising from scratching the itch of your skin disease. The more it itches more you want to scratch to find a momentary relief and pleasure. Being attached to this momentary pleasure that arises from scratching the itch and thus causing more and bigger skin rash is foolish. In reality you are just looking for more causes for your pain and problem.

Actually not having a skin rash is far better than the experience of momentary pleasure from scratching the itch. Trying not to have desire for sensory pleasure that lasts for only a moment is like trying not to have a skin rash at all.

The pleasure of not having a skin rash is greater than the pleasure from scratching the rash. Similarly, the pleasure of not having a clinging desire for sensory pleasures is superior to the temporary pleasure felt from indulging in them. How can this be? Because the absence of a pain that needs relief is a real pleasure in itself. Desiring or attaching to pleasure is pain because you need relief after relief without end.

Therefore, the great eighth century Indian Buddhist master Shantideva said in *A Guide To The Bodhisattva Way Of Life*:

> *There is a momentary pleasure when you scratch the itch. However, an absence of the itch is more pleasurable and superior than the pleasure arising from the scratch.*
>
> *Similarly, there is a momentary pleasure from indulging in the objects of desire. But an absence of desire is more pleasurable and superior than the pleasure arising from the indulgence in the object of desire.*

All forms of desire and attachment to pleasure, and the pleasure that does not last longer than what you ordinarily think or expect are defined as suffering of change. The ordinary pleasure will inevitably decrease and then finally the decrease in pleasure becomes discomfort, which leads to frustration and anger. No one living being is free from this form of suffering. Rich people suffer from mental discomfort, and the poor suffer from physical discomfort.

That is why the great third century Indian Buddhist master Aryadeva rightly said in a short form :

Misery for the rich people is mental, and misery for the poor is physical.

This seems very obviously true.

The third level of suffering—**the suffering of pervasive conditioning**—basically refers to your own psycho-physical existence. Your existence is a product of karma and it is under the control of it. Your existence serves as a basis for the arising of the first two levels of sufferings.

Your existence attracts suffering just as rotten flesh attracts flies to land on it. Your life is fragile in nature, contaminated with karma and delusions, subject to pain at any given moment, subject to all sorts of infection, and a vessel for 424 illnesses.

Your very existence itself is of the nature of suffering since it has the malaise produced by karma. This malaise acts as a seed for your physical discomfort and displeasure. Your mind is infected with delusions. This infection acts as the seed for mental discomfort, distress, irritation, agitation, mental itch and rash, and painful longing and clinging, holding you always in a restless state. There is absolutely no room for inner joy, peace, and serenity that put you in a comfortable and restful state.

These three levels of sufferings cannot cease unless their causes are eradicated. **Karma and the delusions with their underlying root of ignorance are the fundamental causes for these sufferings.** Science and technology cannot help you to eradicate the karma, delusions, and ignorance. Instead science may support the karma and delusions and intensify the causes of human suffering, if the use of science and technology is not based on love, compassion, ethics, and wisdom.

After you carefully consider the various levels of pain and sufferings that have no outside remedy or help, a strong **fear** or a highly disturbed feeling must occur in your mental state. This fear causes you to seek help from whoever has the capability to provide you the solution to end the vicious cycle of samsaric pain and sufferings.

The above mentioned pain and sufferings are general problems of the human realm of samsara. Now we will look at the other samsaric realms, where each individual undergoes suffering according to his or her karma just as in the human realm.

CHAPTER THREE

The Six Realms of Samsara

As we have seen in Chapter Two, there are Four Critical Factors in taking Refuge, the first being the inner causes for taking Refuge. The two most important of these inner causes are fear and lucid faith. Fear of samsaric suffering depends on familiarity with the pain and suffering of all the realms of samsara.

In terms of living beings, there are six types of beings. In terms of realm, there are three levels of realms within the parameters or entirety of samsaric existence.

The six types of living beings are: hell beings, ghosts, animals, humans, jealous beings or Asuras, and celestial beings or Devas. They are classified into two groups—unfortunate and fortunate. The first three beings are unfortunate beings and last three are fortunate beings. This classification is made based on the intensity of the pain and sufferings they feel as well as the length of the period that they go through suffering. The three unfortunate beings have more pain and more intense pain with almost no possibility to have a moment of relief, whereas, the three fortunate beings have less intense pain with an occasional relief which is however still very momentary.

The specific sufferings of hell beings

Hell beings suffer unbearably intense heat or cold that causes painful blisters all over the body. Hell beings frequently become faint from the intense pain over and over, again and again. Their surroundings either are covered with hot lava, blazing fire flame, quicksand-like fire field, burning metal ground, or are covered with freezing ice, snow, wind, and darkness, and there is absolutely no shelter to be found.

Hell beings in the miserable realm suffer from intense heat or cold with no relief. The only thought or desire that they can have is to get out of this miserable realm. They live with this suffering without escape approximately 500 years. The living year in the hell realm is much longer than the human year on earth. Fifty human years equal to the hell being's one day.

In the *Abidharmakosha* Acharya Vasubhandu says:
Fifty human years is a single day for the lower beings like hell.

It is beyond your imagination and comprehension that the hell realm exists but you cannot say that it does not exist— it is not possible to doubt without having a reasonable clue or reasons why it does not exist, and the existence of the hell realm cannot be disproven.

The realm of the ghosts is located above the hell realm. The ghost is a confused and lost spirit but it has a physical body. The ghosts are not harmful by nature but their actions and behaviors often become negative and harmful towards human beings due to their karma. There are some scattered or wandering ghosts living on the earth. A human being who has higher psychic power or due to the karmic link with a particular ghost can actually see the ghost for a very brief moment. Other than that, ghosts in general cannot be seen by your ordinary perception.

The specific sufferings of ghosts or confused and lost spirits

The ghosts are dominated by sufferings of intense hunger and thirst. Their bodies are thin like a skeleton but with a huge belly, tiny throat, and needle-eye size mouth. They see a mirage as water. When they approach the mirage with a hope of finding water, what they see turns out to be just dry sand. They become angry and faint. It happens all the time and they go through this experience of fainting over and over, again and again.

Even if on a very rare occasion they find food and drink, they are unable to consume it due to the hindrances because of their karma. When they approach the food and drink, it turns into pus, rotten blood, and mucus. Or they see a strange being with a terrifying weapon protecting the food or drink. Even in the absence of these two hindrances still they cannot consume food and drink due to their tiny throat and mouth the size of the eye of a needle. They choke and become faint.

Their lips and mouth are very dry and cracked due to intense thirst. They are extremely weak due to hunger but still they are running to look for food and drink throughout the day and night. Ghosts live very long in constant pain and suffering, but not as long as hell beings.

The specific sufferings of animals

Animals are dominated by the sufferings of being killed, tortured, put to work, beaten, and their freedom being controlled by the higher beings like humans. They also feel the suffering and fear of being killed and eaten by one another. Many of the animals are treated as mere objects for human consumption with no respect and protection for their lives. They are being sold here and there by humans. Animals are used as the source of meat, fur, and leather for human comfort and luxury. Also, animals are used for sports just for human pleasure and fun. They are subjected to many painful tools and methods to make them grow bigger and fatter just so that they may be killed for meat and leather.

Animals suffer from being stupid. For instance, a pig is raised with good feed, given baths, kept healthy and patted every day on the shoulder to see how well grown with fat and meat it is. The only reason all this is done is so that the pig is fit to be killed for meat. However, the poor pig thinks that his master loves him so much and is being very kind towards him. The pig does not know that all of these treatments that seem to be good and kind from his perspective are not done for his benefit at all. Because of its stupidity, the pig does not make any effort to run away from being killed one day; therefore the pig suffers from the pain of the butcher's knife.

Many animals are not only put into hard work when they are young and strong, but also are put to sleep when they no longer can work because they are old and weak. We feed them with handfuls of grass and buckets full of water. They get no pay check, no benefits, no retirement security, no pension, and no nursing home to live in when they become old.

Animals are generally treated without respect and without a sense of any compassionate care—except your own pets. Other animals are born, they live and work for the humans, and finally they are killed for meat, fur, and leather. You cherish green grass in your back yard more than the animal life there and their right to live with freedom sharing the world with humans.

Some of the animals like lobsters, crabs, oysters, and mussels are either fried or cooked alive in hot oil or boiling water. Octopus will be killed in a very brutal manner by means of hitting the octopus harshly on the ground many times until it is dead, like a basketball player hitting the ball on the playground over and over until he makes a score. The way the octopus is killed by this brutal means is just for the sake of the taste and texture of the meat for human pleasure. The way these animals are killed and are caused so much intense pain is similar to the karmic effects of the hell realm, but the experience is not as painful and intense in terms of length of the time and repetition of the experience.

Human beings do not allow many of the animals to grow and live in a natural way. Animals are fed with all sorts of chemically processed food and injected with hormones to speed up their growth of more meat and fat. We put a price on their body, on their meat, fur and leather, etc. How would you feel about it if someone were to put a price on your body and advertise it on TV and in the newspaper? No one human being could bear and tolerate it even for a moment. You would be terrified, horrified, and probably would become faint with an intense feeling of anger and ill-treatment. However, human beings do this to animals without having any concern for their well-being, or how they go through pain and suffering.

Two obvious examples that I would like share in this book about the pain and sufferings of animals caused by humans are: in the United States we celebrate the Thanksgiving holiday by killing millions of turkeys and then we congratulate ourselves. We celebrate oyster festivals and oyster-eating contests by killing millions and billions of oysters. We take joy in the pain of animals who do not have protection. Animals in general are destitute, with no protection at all except in a few individual cases.

Another example: we do very painful experiments on animals through various means such as giving poisons to see how their body reacts to a certain poison and what type of damage it causes to their organs. We give them diseases to see whether there can be a cure. We cut their limbs and remove their organs for our scientific experiment. We starve them to death. We not only purposefully give them diseases but we intentionally prolong their pain for our better scientific results.

We do these ill treatments not only for the better understanding of various diseases and for finding out their remedy, but we also do many painful tests on animals just for the production of cosmetics for humans. We cause so much pain to poor animals just for the sake of "beauty" which is deceptive to the eyes of naïve people whom you have never met before. It is deceptive because it is just used to lure or confuse the other person through your artificial handmade beauty with a cosmetic product. The "beauty" made with cosmetics lasts like a snow flake on you; it can be easily washed away by water, your own sweat, and your own angry face and negative attitude.

There may be some good reasons behind these ill treatments towards the animals if the intention behind the act is purely to improve the quality of the understanding of the various diseases and their subtle causes in order to find the ways and means to prevent them and to find their cure. If the intention behind these acts is to make money, or just to fulfill the scientist's ego and fantasy, then these are just heartless brutal acts towards the animals, done because they do not have protection and their life means no more than a piece of meat for your meal or the object of your heartless playful sport.

On moral and ethical grounds, there cannot be any good reason behind the ill treatment of animals if the intention is just to produce cosmetics for money and a superficial sense of your being pretty and good looking in order for you to go out with this sense of yourself as good looking.

To study various lipsticks and eye make-up, experiments are made on animals that cause their lips to get severely burned and their eyes to get swollen; their faces turn to look like a steak cooked on the hot grill.

Don't we see that these are heartless brutal acts towards the animals? Don't we see that this terrible pain is caused by humans solely for unnecessary human comfort, beauty, and luxury? Don't we see that the animals are only used for human consumption and as a source of food to nourish our bodies so that we do more unethical or very unwholesome things on the earth rather than doing good things?

More than forty percent of wild animals in Tibet are already extinct because the Chinese kill them wholesale for meat, fur, and leather to boost their economy. Seventy-five percent of the pure Tibetan mountain dogs no longer exist today. The Chinese breed them too much for bigger and quicker dog production just to make meat for them to eat. This brutal act of China is also part of the worldwide man-caused animal suffering, not just an isolated political interest from the side of China.

The meat and fish industry have developed tools for torturing and killing various animals. They threaten their lives with all sorts of vicious devices—nets, snares, traps, hooks, guns, arrows, knives, etc. In some cases the killing of animals is a slow process in consideration of the taste and tenderness of the meat, etc.

Many animals are killed simply for their horns, fur, skins, tusks, bones, musk. And the rest their body is dumped at dishonorable places like the smelly trash of our kitchen.

The bodies of the animals killed by cars on the highway are treated worse than the trash. We run over the bodies and crush and smash them with no sense of respect and compassionate concern for them.

In brief, animals are subject to limitless pain and suffering just because of being born as animals in the animal realm. Every living being including yourself has a risk and karmic potential to be born in the lower realms in the next life if you fail to regard the natural law of karma.

The specific sufferings of humans

Human beings are considered more fortunate beings with free will, leisure, freedom, and an immense potential to attain everlasting joy and happiness. However, due to our ignorance we misuse our human condition: we look after loved ones only through attachment and we crush our enemies with anger and hatred. Human beings' free will and freedom are not controlled by non-human beings, although some people believe in supernatural forces that control our life and behavior. For all these reasons—free will, leisure, freedom and potential—the human form is considered as a fortunate form.

However, as discussed above, the human form is by no means free of pain and sufferings. There are many human sufferings, for instance the suffering of sickness, old age, and death. Similarly, there are the sufferings of fear: fear of separation from loved ones, fear of leaving behind everything that you possess at the time of death, fear of not knowing where you will end up taking rebirth, fear of losing that self which is deeply seated in your heart and which you cherish so much, and fearful concern about who will take away your wealth.

Firstly you are born with a very fragile body subject to all sorts of external elemental threats. Your body is no more than a piece of meat that needs to be protected from getting rotten or from various insects and flies. Then gradually your body decays and becomes like the dry leaves of the trees in the cold winter season.

At the end of life your body become like a leafless dormant tree in the harsh cold winter. Finally your body is no longer under your control. It is in the control or power of the Lord of Death or *Duy Gyal Dag Po Chee Dak Shin Jey* in Tibetan.

Duy Gyal Dag Po Chee Dak Shin Jey means: you cannot escape or delay your death when the time jumps on you. The moment of death is something that cannot be delayed or prolonged; neither can anything remain exactly the same as it was in the previous moment. Time is one of the most powerful forces that sits behind every thing, exerting unescapable pressure for something new to happen or for nothing new at all to occur.

Other human sufferings are the sufferings of not being able to look after your loved ones, and of not being able to crush your enemies; sufferings when loved ones and friends turn into your enemy; sufferings of insecurity in your relationship and social position.

Also there are the sufferings of discontentment with what you have and the painful urge to get more, bigger, and better with no end. There is the pain of not getting what you desire. Even if you get what you want, still you are unhappy for not getting it in the way you want. There is the pain of not being able to protect what you have, and there is the pain of not being able to get rid of what you do not want.

Similarly, humans feel the sufferings of loneliness, sadness, depression, fear, confusion, and a constant feeling of disturbance or agitation in your mental and psychological state. And humans feel suffering when many of the causes for happiness flip to become the cause for unexpected pain and anxiety.

One of the exclusive sufferings of human beings is unlimited needs, desires, and wants which are impossible to fulfill regardless of who you are and what your capabilities are. The failure to fulfill these unlimited needs and desires alone makes humans always unhappy with a highly disturbing feeling of failure.

The specific sufferings of Asuras or jealous beings

Asuras or jealous beings live high up in space next to the celestial beings. They are dominated by the sufferings of intense jealousy towards the good fortune of celestial beings. Because of their jealousy they often fight with the celestial beings and suffer from being killed, being seriously wounded, and the permanent loss of their limbs.

For the jealous beings, no moment is free from intense dispute, fights, and physical pain from injury.

Regardless of how long and through what means they fight with the celestial beings they will never gain anything at any level. They are the losers forever. However, the fighting with various weapons with the celestial beings will never stop because of the karma of the Asuras. Their karma makes them live and experience these sufferings during their whole life without escape.

The specific sufferings of celestial beings

The celestial beings live a realm with two levels located high in space. The two levels are called *Rupa* and *Arupa* realms. In the Rupa realm the celestial beings have a physical form and in the Arupa realm the beings are formless.

The celestial beings are dominated by the sufferings of having too long a life, and knowing exactly when they are going to die and where they are going to take rebirth.

A majority of the celestial beings will take rebirth in one of the lower realms right after their death. This is because they have completely used up all of their good karma during their long life period. Although they do have the opportunity to create a new good karma during their lifetime as celestial beings, what is left with them at the end of their life is negative karma from their past lives. This negative karma automatically becomes active at their time of death and propels them into a lower realm.

Also, the celestial beings suffer from being abandoned by their loved ones prior to their death. In addition, they suffer from the painful symptoms of their death, such as intense discomfort with their seat and bed, a horrible bad odor coming from their body, the illuminating light vanishing from their body, and watching their flower garland wilting, etc.

They experience these pains and sufferings for seven days of their own time prior to their actual death. However, it is very long compared to our human time. Celestial beings' one day equals to our fifty years—which means they suffer from these pains and sufferings for 350 human years.

No one is free from suffering

In general no one sentient being is free of the general sufferings of samsara and the specific sufferings of a particular rebirth in a different realm. However, the sufferings of fortunate beings—humans, jealous beings or demigods, and celestial beings or happy gods—are less intense and often the beings can have brief relief from their pain. On the other hand, the sufferings of the three unfortunate lower beings—hell beings, ghosts, and animals—are more intense and it is very rare to have a moment of relief from the sufferings, regardless of whether they are physical, mental, emotional, or psychological pain.

Until you are free from being subject to take rebirth in samsara and particularly in one of the lower realms, there is no way for your life to be happy and joyful. From the first moment of your birth until death you naturally go through distress and many discomforts in every moment of your life.

Fear, the first necessary cause of going for Refuge

Because of the heaviness of the negative karma we all carry in our mental continuum, the majority of us are sure to roll down to the lower realms after our death and few of us may climb up towards the higher fortunate realms.

You can judge this for yourself. You indulge in many unwholesome actions and deeds of body, speech, and mind in everyday life. What you do, say, and even think is often motivated by selfish interest without any moral concern for others' well-being or for the ultimate outcome or karmic effect of your action. Your mind is infected with delusions and these make your actions to be highly contaminated with the seed of pain and harmfulness.

Your indulgence in selfish actions is very powerful and the selfish actions are usually fully completed. Indulgence in selfless compassionate actions is much less powerful and in many cases the actions are incomplete and ineffective.

You engage more in:
Killing than in protecting lives
Stealing than in giving and sharing
Sexual misconduct or selfish sexual activity without any sense of love than in making love as an expression of love
Lying with or without reason than in being truthful
Slander with the intention to cause disharmony than in creating harmony for peace
Insulting and harsh speech than in gentle and respectful words
Idle chatter and spreading rumors than in meaningful talk and in maintaining a noble silence when the talk is not necessary
Coveting than in taking joy and delight in others' good fortune
Harboring ill will towards others than in wishing for others to be happy
Holding a wrong view of reality than in openly seeking the truth of what is wholesome versus unwholesome, right versus wrong, virtuous versus non-virtuous, ethical versus unethical, and what is good to be cultivated versus what is bad and to be discarded. Many of you choose to act in the way you personally want and think right at the moment without using the precious gift of your human brain and intelligence to discern the best or most ethical course.

These acts make you to roll down into the lower realms rather than evolve towards a fortunate rebirth in the higher realms. Because of this there is an imminent risk for you to take rebirth in a lower realm after death, and therefore you must feel intense **fear** with a sense of urgency to seek help to avert this risk sooner.

This **fear**, based on the fact of your real knowledge of your own unhealthy actions and deeds as the reason for lower rebirth, **is the first necessary cause of going for Refuge**. It is not a fear of God or Buddha sending you to the hell realm; rather it is a fear of your own actions and deeds—your own karma—sending you into a lower realm. This strong fear opens the door for you to go for Refuge from your heart.

Lucid faith, the second cause of going for Refuge

After searching for someone to be your guide to find the ways and means to stop this relentless cycle of pain and suffering, you will see through your sincere and unbiased mind that the Buddha, his teaching of Dharma, and the Sangha are the unmistaken possible guide. You will be able to recognize the capability of Buddha, Dharma, and Sangha to be your unfailing guide. This recognition should induce joy and trust in your heart like the joy of finding the most rare and precious jewel that ever existed on the earth. This recognition that leads to **lucid faith** with undisputable, unquestionable trust in the Three Jewels is the **second** necessary cause of going for Refuge.

In general there are three types of lucid faith. They are: vivid faith, eager faith, and confident faith. Vivid faith is the faith that inspires you when you think of the good qualities of the Three Jewels and their unfailing capability to help you accomplish your goal.

Eager faith is your strong wish and willingness to be free of the sufferings of samsara in general, and particularly the sufferings of lower realms, and your eagerness to enjoy the happiness of higher realms and liberation. It is also your eagerness to cultivate wholesome actions when you hear what benefits they bring and your willingness to abandon negative actions when you hear what terrible harm and pain they cause.

Confident faith is the faith or trust in the Three Jewels that arises in your heart and which makes you humble, respectful and joyfully hopeful, with the voluntary urge to accept the jewel of Buddha as your unfailing teacher, the jewel of Dharma as your unfailing path, and the jewel of Sangha as your unfailing source of inspiration and determination to move on the path.

You have lucid faith and trust in the Buddha's capability to guide you on the path so that you can protect yourself through practicing what is to be cultivated and what is to be discarded as taught by the Buddha. This faith and trust is surely not just a belief that Buddha will protect you with his own hands or by holding you in his arms without your serious effort in practicing what the Buddha has told you to practice in his wholesome teachings. This lucid faith or trust in Buddha's ability to guide you opens the door to take Refuge.

In order to recognize the capability of the Buddha to be your guide, you must understand the unique qualities of the Three Jewels—the jewel of Buddha, the Dharma, and the Sangha. Without the full understanding of their capabilities and qualities that qualify them to be your unfailing guide, your Refuge will be mere words or blind faith that have no higher spiritual effects.

CHAPTER FOUR

The Objects to Which You Go for Refuge

The objects to which you go for Refuge are the Buddha, the Dharma, and the Sangha. They are known as the three precious jewels or Tri Ratna in Sanskrit. In this chapter I will describe each of the Three Jewels, and in the two subsequent chapters I will discuss each in more detail.

The Jewel of Buddha

The **Buddha** is a fully enlightened being with the inner qualities of limitless love, compassion and wisdom, and an omniscient mind which sees all existing things and phenomena directly without the slightest obstruction.

The Buddha has two unique perfections: the perfection of realization and the perfection of elimination of all obstructions, flaws, and potential for all possible negativities.

The perfection of realization has two main components: compassion and wisdom. Compassion is the unfailing motivating force for Buddha's activities to occur whenever, wherever, and for whomever there is need. Wisdom is the unfailing power for every assistance to become effective and to match with the need of limitless beings whose needs, predispositions, and karmic inclinations are very different and vary widely from one another.

Due to the Buddha's universal love and compassion, he will never abandon anyone or exclude anyone from being helped by him at any time and in any situation. The activities of Buddha's love and compassion are like the sunlight that does not discriminate in terms of where it should shine or not shine on the earth. Similarly, Buddha's love and compassion do not discriminate, do not exclude anyone from being the object of his help.

Due to the Buddha's wisdom, his enlightened activities— including the teachings—cannot be mistaken, flawed, in error, or misleading. Buddha has totally eradicated non-knowingness or ignorance through the realization of wisdom.

The love, compassion, wisdom, and omniscient mind remain active at all times. Because of this the Buddha's activities for helping others will never stop or cease, just as the ocean's waves and currents never stop or cease as long as the world remains. Likewise, the Buddha's enlightened activities will continue timelessly until samsara becomes empty of sentient beings who are subject to pain and sufferings. These are the reasons why the Buddha is trustworthy and qualified to be the object of Refuge.

Also, there are four other reasons that explain why the Buddha is qualified to be the unfailing object of Refuge for those who seek the path to ultimate happiness. The four reasons are:

1. Buddha has mastered himself and attained the sublime state of fearlessness.
2. He is not subject to karma, delusions, obstruction to liberation or obstruction to omniscience, nor is he subject to mental, emotional, and psychological distress or confusion.
3. He has gained the perfection of wisdom and thus he is not subject to imperfection.
4. He is completely skilled in the ways and means of helping others through knowing every detail of the needs, predispositions and karmic inclinations of those he helps. He knows the exact time to act, the very way to act or how to act and what means are to be used for his help to become effective and meaningful.

Buddha has great love and compassion that shine on all living beings equally without room for discrimination. He treats all living beings as his own innocent child with love and compassion, without judging the behavior of his child.

What Buddha really wants for his child and for all living beings is happiness and freedom from pain and sufferings. The Buddha himself takes the responsibility on his own shoulders to make this happen without delay.

He is pleased—not by material offerings and gifts, service, or favor, but by the offerings of your Dharma practice and that you live according to what he teaches, because your serious Dharma practice and living according to his teachings is the true help that the Buddha gives in leading you to the ultimate joy and happiness that cannot be reversed once you have attained it.

Such a being who has these qualities in his or her deep nature is no doubt worthy to be the unfailing object of Refuge for whatever you are attempting to seek and to accomplish.

A Buddha, for example Buddha Shakyamuni, the Buddha of our age or epoch, has all of these qualities and he is the absolutely unmistaken, unfailing, non-misleading object of Refuge as your ultimate guide. You must see and appreciate these qualities in the Buddha in order to take Refuge in him from your humble and undoubting heart.

The *Praise in One Hundred and Fifty* Stanzas, or sTod *Pa Gya Nga Chu Pa Ley* says:

> *The one in whom no fault*
> *Can exist,*
> *The one in whom all excellent qualities*
> *Always exist—*
>
> *If you are sensible and have pith in your heart,*
> *It is correct to go for refuge to just such a person,*
> *To praise, admire, and honor him,*
> *And to abide in his holy teachings.*

The Jewel of Dharma

The second Jewel as the object of Refuge is the **Dharma**.

Dharma in Sanskrit means holy teaching. Dharma is translated as Cho in Tibetan, and means one that brings inner transformation through which one can attain everlasting joy and happiness. Dharma is the sole remedy for the samsaric pain and suffering that have no other means of remedy.

In today's world, many people naively believe that science can alleviate all of human pain and suffering. Such people may take science as their religion and the scientist as their God. This is an absolutely deluded form of naïvety that they live with.

The Dharma is the only thing that has potential to make you peaceful, to reduce the causes and conditions for pain and sufferings, to increase the causes and conditions for joy and happiness, to secure your inner sense of comfort and security, to bring you inner strength and hope, to help you to deal with your own problems without causing problems in your family, community, and society.

One important thing to bear in mind is that the Dharma absolutely helps you to compromise and reconcile the various contradicting thoughts, ideas, and emotions in your mind. That many people in the world commit suicide is primarily due to their failure to reconcile and find a compromise among the many crazy thoughts and emotions in their mental continuum.

Science and technology have no power to help you to secure your sense of inner comfort, security, and hope at the time of death. The final and ultimate thing that science and technology can do for you is to keep you on the ventilator. In some cases that is done as part of a scientific experiment or as a way of generating money from yourself or your loved ones.

It is much wiser and better to rely on Dharma practice than on anything else for your best interests from birth to death. Be fully prepared to accept the reality of death when the time comes. Create merit and virtue through good deeds for the unfailing cause of your joy and happiness in this life as well as in your future lives. How good and happy you will be in the next rebirth is solely within your own hands and effort. At the same time, you can take advantage of science and technology to solve your temporary material problems and discomforts, and for the purposes of convenience in your life.

The Dharma of Lord Shakyamuni Buddha has two levels: Sutrayana and Tantrayana. At the root of both these two levels of teachings are love, compassion, and the firm principle of ahimsa—non-violence. This proves that the Dharma is wholesome, peaceful and holy, and that it must be used solely for peace, joy, and happiness for all living beings.

The Dharma consists of three factors which are necessary tools for attaining enlightenment or at least the higher and most reliable form of inner joy and happiness. The three factors are: **ethics, meditation, and wisdom**. These three factors must be nurtured, cultivated and practiced within the healthy soil of love and compassion in your heart.

Ethics is practiced by a highly trained mind that naturally abstains from every possible negative or harmful action or deed in all times, conditions, and places. It is the cause for developing all that is good, virtuous, and wholesome. It is the fundamental base for spiritual training and realization. Ethics is the one that secures your own happiness as well as the happiness of all others. Proper practice of ethics makes your actions very gentle and subdued, and non-threatening to anyone's well-being.

Meditation is a process of training your mind in order for the mind to become calm, peaceful, serene and focused, with more room for inner joy and contentment. It is all about ways and means for gaining full control over your mind and using it in the way you want at any time. Meditation sharpens the mind and expands its awareness. It helps to treat the mind's delusional infection and to make the mind extremely healthy with a strong immunity to resist the negative effects of thoughts and emotions.

Long training in meditation surely leads to penetrative insight into the deep nature of reality and helps to eradicate all confusion, misperception, and delusory thoughts and emotions from their subtle germinal seed.

Through the long process of training in meditation based on correct instruction by a qualified and experienced teacher, you will no doubt attain a happy and peaceful mind that is steady and reliable.

You will become one of the happiest persons on the earth with an inner mental wealth of love, compassion, peace, joy, serenity, and the wisdom that will be the strength of your heart. What a wonderful thing you can accomplish by relying in the guidance of Buddha and practicing his teachings, the Dharma!

Wisdom is a quality of a highly sharp mind with deep focus which perceives the true nature of all things and phenomena directly without need of intellectual theory or description. The most refined and pure form of wisdom is the wisdom realizing the emptiness of all things.

The true nature of all things is that they lack inherence, or inherent existence. What things are and how things come into being is the result of causes and conditions. Nothing is causeless or independently existing. Thus things do not have room for inherence although they can appear to exist independently as a table, cup, etc. Table, cup, etc. are labels or designations for things that are the products of their causes and conditions and that are the sum of their parts. However, things can have the functional ability to fulfill conventional needs and necessity although they lack any form of essential quality or inherence.

Wisdom is that which perceives the emptiness of all things without having a conflicting confusion between the empty nature and the functional ability of things and phenomena.

The way things exist is like an incredibly beautiful rainbow. A rainbow has the ability to be beautiful but it completely lacks any inherent beauty that can be found either in the rainbow itself or wherever the rainbow was formed. The beauty of the rainbow that induces joy in your mind has no contradiction with the rainbow's lack of inherent beauty—the way the rainbow really is.

Similarly, wisdom sees the empty nature of all things but it accepts their functional utility and beauty since there is no contradiction between an object's empty nature and its functionality and beauty.

Because of wisdom, your mind steadily remains calm, peaceful and serene, without a need or uncontrollable inner urge for you to feel either attraction or repulsion.

Again, I am inspired to say: what a beautiful thing you can accomplish by relying on the guidance of the Buddha and practicing his teachings!

The Dharma is 1. the collection of teachings to be practiced properly and 2. ultimately the realizations to be attained through the Dharma practice. You practice in order that the realizations will occur. If the Dharma would be only the teachings, the texts, then you could sleep in the library!

Dharma, or teachings, is not a series of instructions forcing you to believe and to follow out of blind faith without a legitimate reason in your own mind for accepting the Dharma with a sense of joy and trust in its working power to overcome suffering and attain happiness.

The Dharma—the teaching of the Lord Buddha—is based on indisputable reason and fact. Therefore, the more you reflect, contemplate, meditate, and examine with your sharpest mind, the more you will find the teachings to be fact-based, and the more you will realize that the Dharma is completely flawless and reliable so that you can practice it wholeheartedly. This will automatically lead you to confirm that the Buddha is the teacher of supreme truth and the most worthy one to rely on for guidance.

The Dharma can be classified into two: the holy scriptural texts which contain the teachings, and the realizations acquired through practicing those teachings. Holy scriptural texts written in Sanskrit, Pali, Tibetan, Hindi, etc. are the immediate source of knowledge and wisdom, and the Buddha is the ultimate source. There are 108 volumes of Buddha's own words and 225 volumes of commentary written by the Arhats not long after Buddha's passing into Parinirvana. All together there are 333 volumes of holy scriptural texts. These are the completely flawless body of the Buddhist teachings, and they are absolutely reliable since the entire meaning of the teachings is based on the supreme truth.

The Dharma of the scriptural texts is a relative object of Refuge but not the ultimate object of Refuge. **The ultimate object of Refuge is the realizations attained by practicing the Dharma according to the texts.** All the holy texts must be treated with deep respect and viewed as an actual speech or teaching of the Buddha expounding the truth of reality.

The Dharma of the actual realization occurs from the long practice of thoroughly familiarizing yourself with the teachings and internalizing them in your heart and mind. This acquired realization through vigorous practice is the actual Dharma that is the ultimate object of Refuge because the realization acquired within your heart and mind is the one that protects you from the samsaric pain and sufferings. This realization can only occur in you if you cherish the Buddha as an ultimate source of virtue, place your wholehearted trust in his guidance and practice his teachings with single-minded, one-pointed effort and firm decision from you heart.

You can inspire yourself by taking as examples the great yogi Milarepa and Jey Lama Tsongkhapa Lobsang Drakpa. These great yogis were able to reach enlightenment in a single lifetime through their firm decision and the strength of their effort motivated by universal love, compassion, and an altruistic intention, accompanied by their strong belief in Satyagraha, the implacable insistence on truth.

It is a bold decision not to give up the truth regardless of how painful, harsh, and long is the process of searching for the truth. In the case of practicing the Dharma, there is the truth of attaining enlightenment based on human potential and intelligence.

It is certain that you will attain enlightenment either in this life or in the next few subsequent lives if you are able to adopt the lifestyle and discipline showed by Milarepa and Jey Tsongkhapa. Their lifestyle and discipline are as stated by Gyal Wa Ayen Sa Pa Chenpo, who was a student or disciple of Tsongkhapa:

> *Like the great yogi Milarepa in the past, and*
> *Jey Lobsang Drakpa in the present.*
> *Except keeping the minimum basic needs for their temporary survival,*
> *All other things like wealth, name, fame, and superficial good image are totally abandoned (through seeing them as a poison).*
>
> *By adopting this simple lifestyle and discipline,*
> *Abiding in the place of solitude (the place that is abandoned by the worldly beings).*
> *And being free from attachment and aversion (because the place in which they live is free of what ordinarily serves as an object of attraction and repulsion).*
> *Putting one pointed effort to extract the essence of human life in every moment.*

And, finally he says:

> *May I be blessed too with this lifestyle in order to extract the essence of human potential.*

You yourself, like Gyal Wa Ayen Sa Pa Chenpo, can make at least a strong wish or prayer to be able to adopt Milarepa and Tsongkapa's lifestyle in order to extract the essence of your precious human life.

Your own pure Dharma practice relying on the guidance of the Buddha will be the only help at the darkest part of your life, i.e. your death. Nothing else can be found to be helpful to secure your inner sense of comfort and to lessen your fear and confusion. Asking prayers and mantras from others is better than nothing but gives no certainty of being helpful to your needs. Therefore, the Lord Buddha Shakyamuni says: *"You are your own protector but nothing outside of yourself can protect you."*

While you have the freedom, opportunity and mental and physical capability, and since you have met with the right guide and the wholesome teachings, you must not miss this golden chance to practice the Dharma and to create merit from your virtuous actions and deeds in everyday life.

You must make sure not to depart into next life with bare empty hands and a mind filled with the seeds for all possible unavoidable pain and sufferings. For you to accomplish this essential task of practicing the Dharma, you must rely solely on the strength of Refuge in your heart.

The Jewel of Sangha

The third jewel as the object of going for Refuge is the **Sangha.** In general the Sangha is a spiritual community established by the Buddha as a rich field of virtue and merit, and as a sphere of Dharma teachings and practice. It is the sphere of teaching, practice, inspiration, determination, and wish to practice with no room to be lazy and prone to seek pleasure in idleness.

It is a field for the lay community to make merit through the practice of making offerings, paying homage and respect, prostration, doing services for the monks and nuns, rennovating temples and holy stupas, receiving blessings and Dharma instructions, asking prayers and pujas for the benefit of deceased and ill beings, and holding and viewing the community of monks and nuns as a source of teachings and realizations.

However, the chief among the Sangha members are those persons who are noble beings, Arya in Sanskrit and Phakpa in Tibetan. Arya means superior. Phakpa means gone beyond the ordinariness. The Sangha in whom you go for Refuge must be the noble or Arya beings. They must have attained the path of seeing, have gained direct realization of emptiness and have perfected the uncontrived love and compassion. Their whole being is in the sphere of Dharma teachings, practices, and virtue.

The Sangha as the object of Refuge has many qualifications. Some of these qualifications are:

The individual Sangha members must teach the Dharma, practice it, contemplate it and meditate on it wholeheartedly. As the teachings' sphere, the Sangha uphold the Dharma, and entrust themselves to the Dharma. The Sangha respect and pay homage to the Dharma from the depths of their humble hearts.

It is the Sangha who perform the Dharma activities, and they are the most admiring and devoted practitioners of the holy teachings. The individual Sangha member is naturally honest, sincere, and humble, is endowed with the quality of love and compassion, and has true compassion as the pith of his or her heart. He or she is always absorbed in the Dharma and always doing good and wholesome practices that awaken others' hearts.

In this degenerate time it may be rare and difficult to find Sangha members who have all of these exalted qualities. But it is more than enough for you if you can find the Sangha with at least one third of these qualities to qualify as an object of Refuge.

It is clear that there are two levels of Sangha: the ultimate Sangha and the relative Sangha. The ultimate Sangha are the noble beings who possess higher realizations and do not have faults which may discourage other practitioners. The relative Sangha are the ordained monks and nuns whose sole performances are giving teachings to others and practicing the teachings purely. Though they may not have actual realization, they at least have the strong experience of the taste of actual realization if their effort does not roll down due to the force of Mara and the temptation of sensual pleasures to which all beings are deeply habituated from their beginningless life.

The Sangha that consists of four or more fully ordained monks or nuns are the relative Sangha, and not the actual object of Refuge. They are a relative object of Refuge, respect, and reverence, because they are the source of prayers, blessings, and an ocean of virtue and merit that benefits countless beings.

The relative Sangha are on their way to become noble beings who are the actual ultimate Sangha, the true object of Refuge. However, the relative Sangha—which primarily refers to those members of the communities of fully ordained monks and nuns—may have some ordinary faults which may discourage or confuse your mind so that you do not feel respectful and reverent toward them. As a serious practitioner you are better to leave their faults aside unless these faults fall into being directly contradictory to Buddha's teachings and therefore act as poison to the Dharma and its practitioners.

Relative Sangha, generally referring to fully ordained monks and nuns, are the ones from whom you can learn good and wholesome things during your lifetime. They are the ones who can help you, through their prayers and comforting wise guidance and advice at the time of death or in other difficult situations when you don't know what to do. So, treating monks and nuns with disrespect or as no more than any ordinary person is, honestly, a serious mistake.

Of course, all the monks and nuns are not perfect, but they are trying their best to follow in the footsteps of the Buddha, the Bodhisattvas, and the other highly realized practitioners. No monk or nun can be found who has no special good qualities deep down in their heart and mind.

Jowo Jey Palden Atisha says:

> *A person who wears the robe with the color of red, maroon, saffron or yellow is sure to have special good qualities in their nature. You must be respectful and be humble to the monks and nuns regardless of their external behaviors. There is a gain for yourself in doing this.*

Whenever Atisha saw a piece of red, maroon, or saffron cloth he immediately picked it up and put it over his head with deep respect. Then he placed it in a clean and safe place. He was doing this through seeing the exalted qualities of 1. the relative Sangha and their role in his spiritual practice and 2. the ultimate Sangha as the object of Refuge for all liberation seekers.

Unfortunately in today's world, more and more people see the monks and nuns as a social burden, as people who for their own comfort and convenience selfishly run away from leading the household life. Also, some people view monks and nuns as failures among human society who have grouped themselves together to survive at the householders' expense. China said in the 1950s and even still says today that the monks and nuns are the blood suckers of human society, and that they are the poison of human society.

There are even people who, while they do not view the monks and nuns like this, view the Sangha as a particular profession similar to the military, social work, or ritual and ceremonial business, and as some religious effigy or lure to entice others to support their survival. Such people's minds are troubled by their own wrong understanding of what it means to be a monk or a nun, and what a monk or nun really is.

Of course, it is easy to see the imperfect part of people but very difficult to see the good part. Your perceptions are heavily habituated with seeing bad in others but not their good part. You always regard your perception as more valid and correct than anything else. You always believe in what you personally think is right or wrong without carefully examining the quality of your own mind and perception. This is the fundamental cause for seeing the Sangha—monks, nuns, and serious practitioners—as no more than anyone else.

CHAPTER FIVE

The Objects to Which You Go for Refuge: Buddha

You go for Refuge knowing the unfailing spiritual qualities of the Buddha, the Dharma and the Sangha. Therefore we will expand considerably on the qualities of the Three Jewels described in the last chapter.

The spiritual qualities of the **Buddha** can be explained in four sub-topics:

1. The qualities of the Buddha's body
2. The qualities of the Buddha's speech
3. The qualities of the Buddha's mind
4. The qualities of the Buddha's enlightened activities

The outstanding qualities of the Buddha's body

The qualities of the Buddha's body are as taught in the *Praise in Honor of One Worthy of Honor*:

Your body, adorned with the signs,
Is beautiful, an elixir for the eyes;
It is like a cloudless autumn sky
Decorated with clusters of stars.

O great Teacher, even the full moon
Free of clouds cannot compare
With the radiant orb of your face
Free of the embellishment of ornaments.

Should a bee see
The lotus of your face
And a lotus opened by the sun,
The bee would wonder which was the real lotus.

Oh ... One so worthy of offerings of trust, your right hand,
Adorned with the sign of the sacred wheel,
Makes the gesture of relief
To living beings terrified by the terror of samsara.

When you recall these qualities of the Buddha's body with your unbiased mind you will surely feel great admiration, uplifted trust, faith, devotion, and respect. You will have a joyful eagerness to follow him to learn the sacred way that leads to having such an unusual stunning body that puts anyone who sees it in a most amazed state.

Since the detailed qualities of the Buddha's body can be found in my book *Essential Ethics* I would avoid repeating here.

The good qualities of the Buddha's speech

The qualities of the Buddha are beyond an ordinary being's imagination. His speech is extremely gentle, soothing, pleasing, calming and undistorted in all time and space. His speech naturally carries the power of truthfulness and subduedness.

The Buddha's single word can explain everything and instantly can be understood by all beings in their own languages. His speech or voice can reach as far as needed. The volume of his voice will be exactly the same to one who is right next to the Buddha and one who is far distant from the Buddha, which means both persons can hear it exactly the same way.

The *Chapter of the Truth* says:

It is like this:
If all living beings simultaneously
Ask questions using many different expressions,

The Buddha understands them in a single moment,
And with a single word gives answers to each.

Similarly the *Praise in One Hundred and Fifty Verses* says:

Your speech, like a rain cloud,
Settles the dust of attachment;
Like the mystical bird Garuda,
It expels the snake of anger.

Because you see the truth, your speech never misleads;
Since it is flawless, it is always correct;
Since it is well-composed, it is easy to understand.
Your words are well-spoken.

At first your speech
Captivates the listeners' mind;
Then if they give it thought,
It clears away delusions.

Your speech delights the learned,
Improves the minds of the less intelligent,
And dispels the darkness of stupidity.
This speech is medicine for all living beings.

Your face is so captivating
But listening to your pleasant speech,
Is still far more joyful.
To all, it appears as a nectar
Flow from the bright moon.

In general there are sixty good qualities of the Buddha's speech mentioned in a various Sutric and Tantric texts. I make effort to mention some of these good qualities here since it is related to our topic, Refuge. The Buddha's speech is

Profound like thunder
Sweet and soothing to the ear
Pleasing and joyful to the mind
Completely clear and audible
Appealing to listen to and without contradiction

Subduing

Instantaneous without repetition

Thoroughly complete

Satisfying to all the senses

Without a pause between the words

Always understandable to whoever hears it

Steady and balanced

Clear and straightforward with no room for confusion or misunderstanding

Reaching as far as needed without losing its initial strength

With natural power to make the listener's mind peaceful and focused

With power to fulfill the needs of each individual living being as a flower rich with pollen fulfills the bee

With power to uplift the minds of all beings

With power to avert the negative forces

With power to increase the positive energy and conducive atmosphere

With power to attract the attention of all beings and provide relief

When you reflect on the good qualities of the Buddha's speech you will certainly have a feeling of joy and respect. You will become closer to his teachings and see that it is worthwhile to learn and practice the teachings wholeheartedly.

The good qualities of the Buddha's mind

There are two main good qualities of the Buddha's mind. They are the quality of caring with great compassion and the quality of all-pervading wisdom . The great compassion is an unforgettable feeling of the unbearable-ness of others' sufferings, with a voluntary wish to help them and to release them from their pain and suffering, and with a deep sense of urgency for this to happen.

Because of his great compassion, Buddha's activities for helping living beings will never end, just as the waves and currents of the great ocean never end until nature no longer needs the great ocean on the earth.

The caring quality of the Buddha with great compassion is like that of a most loving, caring, and compassionate mother who takes care of her innocent child in every single moment by making sure that the child is doing well, is comfortable, and does not lack attention or food or drink. Buddha is like the compassionate mother who helps her child fall asleep by holding it in her warm, soft, secure, and comfortable arms or lap and who delights in providing the child all possible sense of comfort and safety that are within her range of capability and power.

The Buddha's love and great compassion function like the natural energy of the great ocean. The natural energy of the ocean constantly causes waves and currents to arise as the sole activities of the great ocean. There cannot be an ocean which does not create waves and currents on its surface. Similarly, the love and great compassion of the Buddha always generate energy within the realm of Dharma Kaya and cause enlightened activities to arise timelessly. There cannot be a Buddha who does not perform enlightened activities timelessly since the needs of the living beings are there timelessly.

The *Chapter Of the Truth Speaker* says:

The supreme sage feels great compassion
When he sees beings whose minds
Are constantly obscured by the dark gloom of ignorance,
Locked in the prison of samsara.

The sage's compassion arises spontaneously;
It is impossible for it not to do so.
The Buddha is free of faults because he is concerned
With the needs of all sentient beings.

Wisdom is the mind realizing all knowable things instantaneously and directly, like seeing a small piece of crystal in the palm of the hand. The Buddha's wisdom not only makes him see things directly and clearly, but also makes him see through things as if they would be transparent, without leaving any part unseen. Because of this wisdom, the Buddha's help can in no way become ineffective or fruitless.

Buddha can see clearly through his wisdom eye things such as when to act, how to act, the place to act, through what means to act, through what words and actions to act, through what message to act, and through what manner and behavior to act in order for his help to perfectly match with the real needs and wants of the recipients of his help.

The Buddha's mind sees the two levels of the truth simultaneously. The truths are: relative truth and ultimate truth. The relative truth is all that which appears to a dualistic mind and which functions to fulfill conventional needs and necessity. It refers to the truth of how things appear and how they are capable to function in terms of how they act as a basis for generating various feelings and experiences of joy or sadness and pleasure or pain. This relative or conventional truth lies within the relative everyday things and objects. One cannot deny its validity or existence, at least within the realm of the conventional world.

The ultimate truth is the subtle mode and manner in which all things actually exist as opposed to how they appear to a dualistic mind. Things and objects appear to a dualistic mind as being intrinsically existing and capable to function, as if seen solely from the objective viewpoint and as if their appearance had nothing to do with the subjective point of view.

The way things and objects appear is totally different from the way they actually exist. The way things appear is the relative truth, and the way things actually exist is the ultimate truth. However, the relative truth and the ultimate truth are not unrelated. They are the two sides of the same coin, or they are the two different perspectives on the same thing.

In order for the Buddha's mind to know things he does not need the support of any name, term, description, definition, or pre-thinking. His knowledge is instantaneous without any time gap or delay between what is to be known and the knower.

The *Praise in Honor of One Worthy of Honor* says:

Only your sublime wisdom
Comprehends all things of knowledge;
For everyone other than you
There are things yet to be known.

Oh ... Buddha, the entire origination
Of all types of phenomena throughout time
Is within the range of your mind,
Like a Kyurura fruit in the palm of your hand.

The good qualities of the Buddha's enlightened activities

The enlightened activites are known as Samudacara in Sanskrit. Samudacara means virtuous activities that have flown or come from the higher consciousness by spiritual force. It is proper to say that Samudacara is like grace in other religious traditions, but it is not grace from God. Rather it is a virtuous activity of the enlightened being's body, speech, and mind.

Due to the force of love and compassion which never ceases to function in the mind of the Buddha, virtuous activities flow and shower down from his body, speech, and mind upon the living beings to provide relief from pain and sufferings.

This virtuous activitiy of the Buddha causes your spiritual practice to be extremely effective and powerful. It pacifies the negative obstructions and activates positive conditions in you so that whatever you do becomes productive and fruitful.

It facilitates the growth of all good and positive seeds, and it helps them to germinate, leading them to to bear their excellent fruits. Buddha's grace is not a one way traffic. It is a two way traffic: one traffic from Buddha's side and the other traffic from your side.

The healthy seed and full openness of mind are required on your side. Only then will the enlightened activities which are the shower of virtuous energy or stimulation occur from the Buddha's body, speech, and mind. This shower will surely ripen the seed and assist it to germinate with a strong and healthy spiritual sprout.

When there are no healthy seed and no full openness of mind from your side, then the Buddha's shower of energy will not work to grow anything in you. It is similar to when one wishes to grow a plant but has no seed, or the seed is rotten, or damaged. The seed will never germinate and grow though the rain showers on the earth from the Dharma Kaya like a vast and boundless sky.

The reason why in that case nothing will grow although rain showers fall on the earth is because a healthy seed is lacking, like the lack of the seed and the openness of mind on your side.

The Buddha's enlightened activities like a shower occur timelessly, but due to the lack of the seed and the openness of mind on your side, no good qualities sprout and take root in your heart and mind. You remain in the dry season, without any fresh things starting and growing to make your life pleasant, happy with freshness, and free of the unhappy feelings of the dry season.

By recalling the enlightened activities of the Buddha you must make sure to have a healthy seed in your heart and to work on opening your mind and heart as a necessary basis for the Buddha's activities to enter and effectively ripen your mind for bearing the fruits of enlightenment.

Let's say that you need the sunlight to nourish your body and to bring your mind into an uplifted state for you to have a sense of joy. But if you choose to stay inside a dark building or under an umbrella that blocks the sunlight from touching and penetrating you, you will never be benefited by the sunlight that shines everywhere on the earth without bias or exception. Now the question is: whose fault is this? Yours or the sun's? Many of you might wrongly blame the sun, which never fails to give you or to make available to you nourishment through its light.

In the same way, the Buddha will never fail to guide you, help you, protect you, nourish you and assist you to grow on the path to enlightenment, if you do not close your mind and if you do not fail to cherish the seed or potential. Actualizing your spiritual potential is more important than any other task.

Reflect on the enlightened activities of the Buddha as stated in the *Praise in One Hundred and Fifty Stanzas:*

Oh Compassionate one, wishing to help,
You care for the benefit of living beings.
How could there be something helpful
Which you have not done?

And the *Praise in Honor of One Worthy of Honor* says:

What trouble is there away from which
You cannot lead living beings?
What excellent thing is there
That you cannot bestow on the world?

You must make yourself fully aware of the enlightened qualities of the Buddha (explained in four sub-topics as seen above) in order that you may develop a deep sense of sincere closeness with Buddha, with the spiritual aspiration to follow him and his teachings so that you can become like him. This is why you take Refuge in the Buddha.

CHAPTER SIX

The Objects to Which You Go For Refuge: Dharma and Sangha

The good qualities of the Dharma or sacred teachings

Once you see the Buddha's enlightened qualities and feel deep admiring trust in the Buddha to be your unfailing guide, you should then reflect on the good qualities of the Dharma or his sacred teachings.

The Buddha possesses boundless good qualities, all of which came from meditating on and realizing profoundly the nature of the human condition and the true nature of reality. The Buddha taught the Dharma—the verbal teachings—and he himself practicesd those teachings thereby attaining realization and those good qualities that result from internalizing the teachings. He gave up all of his pleasure, comfort, worldly elegance and royal luxuries to meditate, through which he discovered and then put into practice the precepts which he taught. That is, he actualized the true cessations, thereby eradicating all obstructions. He meditated on the true path, thereby giving rise to all good qualities which now you admire, and to which you go for Refuge and pay homage.

The Buddha's infinite and boundless good qualities, which you cannot fully imagine with your ordinary mind, arise from the Dharma and its proper practice. The teaching creates and governs these good qualities. They arise from the Dharma and are within the scope of the Dharma. They depend upon the Dharma, and the Dharma produces these good qualities.

The Dharma never fails you in the attainment of your goal of everlasting happiness through a wholesome path. It stops the stream of cyclic existence and clears away the delusions. The Dharma does not mislead those who wish for liberation. It is completely virtuous, and clears away all confusions and wrong view.

The Dharma has absolutely no room to mislead anyone. It comes from an altruistic motivation and profound wisdom with the sole purpose of guiding all living beings on the path to happiness.

The Dharma teaches the supreme truth, virtue, wholesomeness and the joyful method as the only way to true happiness that is not subject to be reversed and is not dependent on external circumstances.

The Dharma is virtuous in nature since it necessarily leads to joy and happiness as its natural result without any possibility for something other than joy and happiness to be its result.

The Dharma is wholesome in its nature since it closes the door to harmfulness.

The Dharma is the ultimate source of knowledge and good qualities that attract others and dim their ego.

In brief, the Dharma is a teaching of the Buddha which shows the ways and methods to work on creating the indispensable inner cause for attaining the everlasting joy and happiness which is the sole purpose of life.

The good qualities of the Sangha or spiritual community

The jewel of Sangha has qualities which act as the true source of inspiration, courage, determination, and strong wish to practice and live according to the Dharma teachings.

The Sangha are the ones from whom you can get help through their sincere prayers and good thoughts.

They have inner good qualities which exhibit to ordinary eyes that realization and enlightenment can possibly be attained by anyone through the serious practice by relying on Buddha's guidance.

There are eight great qualities of the jewel of Sangha. They are

Quality of full realization of the ultimate truth of reality
Quality of full realization of the relative truth of conventional reality
Quality of knowing the variety of aspects of the phenomena
Quality of this knowledge being part of themselves
Quality of freedom from alluring delusions
Quality of freedom from obstructive hindrances or impeding obstructions

Quality of freedom from minor obstructions

Quality of freedom itself which ensures the attainment of enlightenment in the subsequent lives without falling back

The Sangha beings who have these great qualities, whether they are monk, nun, or lay, are the actual jewel of Sangha to whom you go for Refuge—the ultimate Sangha. This jewel of Sangha is ordinarily represented by the community of ordained monks and nuns who keep the vows, practice the Dharma, are always absorbed in doing virtuous deeds, and abide with a joyful and contented attitude. They are neither too excited or elated about good things nor too sad and depressed about unfortunate things.

You can understand the truth and the validity of the Dharma and its practice by reflecting on the qualities of the jewel of Sangha as well as on the ordinary monks, nuns, and serious lay practitioners. This will inspire in you the sincere wish to practice the Dharma and live according to the teachings.

The more you practice the Dharma and the more you gain understanding and realization, the happier you become, with a sense of joy, contentment, a wholesome lifestyle, and gentleness and compassion towards others. This is how the jewel of Sangha is worthy to be the object of Refuge.

Once you fully comprehend the great qualities of the jewel of Buddha, the jewel of Dharma, and the jewel of Sangha, then you are able to go for Refuge by means of recalling their admirable qualities day and night. You go for Refuge in the jewel of Buddha by recalling his enlightened qualities, joyfully and openly accepting the Buddha as the flawless compassionate human teacher of supreme truth and never abandoning reliance on him as your spiritual guide.

You go for Refuge in the jewel of Dharma, the peaceful path to the peaceful result, on which your burning desires are cooled and which allows love, compassion, and wisdom to grow. You take Refuge in the Dharma as the sole path to fulfill the human potential of attaining enlightenment for the sake of all living beings, firmly committing and devoting yourself to the teachings and their practice.

You go for Refuge in the jewel of Sangha, those who have attained higher spiritual realization, as a source of inspiration for the strong wish to practice the Dharma. You see the jewel of Sangha as the most important visible example for you follow to walk on the path and not be discouraged.

Also, the example of the Sangha prevents you from being taken away from the Dharma by the bad influence of deluded beings. You will be protected from the many unnecessary pains and sufferings in this life. More importantly, you will be protected from being born into the lower realms with their greater terrors of samsara.

You can have a strong, firm wish to practice Dharma supported by the valid reasons. No one can cause you to lose your wish to practice and divert you toward a non-Dharmic lifestyle with drinking, taking drugs, spending too much time in the bar, idle chitchat, parties, being always preoccupied with worldly plans and projects which never end until your last breath, buying and shopping for false pleasures and greed, hanging out in the mall and other bustling places and doing other things that gratify your desires and lust—and then living with a deep sense of dissatisfaction and self-annoyance.

CHAPTER SEVEN

The Proper Way You Go for Refuge

There are several proper ways to take Refuge in the Three Jewels.

1. You go for Refuge by knowing the unique spiritual qualities of the Three Jewels—the Jewel of Buddha, the Jewel of Dharma, and the Jewel of Sangha. The unique qualities of the Three Jewels (discussed above) clearly show the distinction between the Three Jewels and non-Buddhist doctrines and their authorities.

Based on your personal understanding and your rights of religious freedom you can make your own voluntary decision to take Refuge in the Three Jewels. You must not attempt to take Refuge under the influence of someone else or just so you can seem to be something special with a new belief that you really don't know about and don't know what to do with.

Rather you must take Refuge after clearly knowing and understanding the distinction between the Buddhist teachings and non-Buddhist teachings, especially the distinction between the Three Jewels and the notion of a God as the ultimate judge of all. This way of taking Refuge is known as "taking Refuge by knowing the distinctions between" the Three Jewels and the non-Buddhist teachings.

2. You can go for Refuge in the Three Jewels through commitment supported by understanding. Going for Refuge through commitment means making a serious and firm promise to uphold the Buddha as the teacher of supreme

truth, the Dharma as the actual path, and the Sangha as your unconditional assistant on the path to attain enlightenment. Enlightenment is the final and ultimate Refuge.

Enlightenment is the final and ultimate Refuge because when you attain the enlightenment primarily through your own practice by following the guidance and instructions of the Buddha, then you are permanently protected from the terrors of samsara. Therefore, the Three Jewels are the first or more indirect Refuge, and enlightenment is the ultimate or direct Refuge. However, without having an indirect Refuge when you are starting out or are still on the path to enlightenment, the ultimate or direct Refuge can by no means be attained.

This sincere and humble way of accepting the Buddha as the unfailing teacher, the Dharma as the unfailing path, and the Sangha as the unconditional supporter for you to move on the path to enlightenment is known as "going for Refuge through commitment."

3. You can go for Refuge in the Three Jewels through seeing that there is no need for any additional thing besides the Three Jewels for your spiritual journey to enlightenment to be complete and fulfilled. To go for Refuge in this way you must not have any sense of needing something else to complete the Three Jewels as your object of Refuge.

You must be very comfortable with the Three Jewels as the sole object of Refuge, comfortable with the knowledge that the Three Jewels are complete without missing anything to help fulfill your goal. You uphold the Three Jewels as the most precious thing in your own heart and live according to their teachings and follow their guidance.

It is like building a holy temple in your own heart. Do your practice with the beauty of the temple in your heart. Do not look for another temple or feel hatred towards other temples and other teachings that do not accord with the qualities of the Three Jewels.

Hold the Three Jewels in your heart as your unfailing guide and do not have any sense of needing to look for any additional thing to complete the Three Jewels, and do not hate or look down on the non-Buddhist teachings and teachers.

This way of upholding the Three Jewels as your precious guide and cherishing them with deep respect, trust, devotion, faith and humility is known as "going for Refuge through the thought of not needing anything" other than the Three Jewels to complete your goal.

It is similar to a healthy marriage, a love bond between two people, a couple. Let us say, you choose a woman from the middle of the thousands of galaxies as your wife through genuine love. Or you select a man from the middle of the thousands of galaxies as your husband through genuine love, not with a lustful fantasy. And then you give your heart to her or him through knowing why you are giving and the reason to give. Finally you get married with her or him with trust, loyalty, faithfulness, respect, and firm commitment to live with with the bond of love. You will find true meaning and purpose in that married life and the marriage fulfills your needs and goal.

Since you are very content with the truth of the meaning of your marriage, you do not have any sense of needing someone in addition to your husband or your wife to make your life happy and to accomplish the goal of what you are looking for on the worldly level.

At the same time you are not seeing others as useless, bad, negative, wrong, or as something to be hated or to be afraid of. You still treat others with respect and in a humble way.

Similarly, you must not hate or disrespect non-Buddhist teachings and preachers when you yourself take Refuge in the Three Jewels, although you yourself are a Buddhist and live according the Buddha's teachings.

In brief, Refuge is the foundation stone for accomplishing the highest spiritual goal that you can achieve through your human potential by combining the mutual work of the good heart and the smart mind.

To repeat: when you take Refuge, voluntarily and openly accepting the Buddha as the flawless teacher, the Dharma as the unfailing path, and the Sangha as the unconditional source of inspiration and courage, you accept them from your heart and not just by words.

You have firmly made the irreversible decision not to give up the Three Jewels as your guide until you attain full enlightenment. You are sure and clear that you don't need any path, teachings, teacher or inspiration other than the Three Jewels.

You have made this decision strongly and firmly in your heart through knowing that the Three Jewels are complete and unfailing for your needs and for accomplishing the goal of liberation or enlightenment.

You uphold the Three Jewels as the foundation stone of the entire Buddhist path, as the source of virtue and merit and as worthy of trust, respect, faith and devotion. The Three Jewels are the source of blessings and boons, the source of joy, happiness, and all other goodness, and the Refuge of this life and the next rebirth. The Three Jewels teach the wholesome ways to live in this life and lead you into the peaceful transition between the Bardo (the intermediate or transitional state after death) and your next rebirth with the light of their wisdom and compassion.

Make sure that you understand the good qualities of the Three Jewels and the Refuge precepts to be observed in order to make the firm decision to take formal Refuge from a qualified lama or guru.

Do not take Refuge lightly

Taking Refuge is not like hastily getting married with someone because of lust and selfish interest and without love and commitments. This type of marriage has no single good meaning or purpose in your life. It only serves as the cause for headache and bitter divorce sooner or later.

This is primarily due to getting married out of lust and selfish interest without ever being serious about living with the marriage commitments from the very day of your marriage with the one that you chose. It is completely wrong to make the decision to get married with someone if you are not serious about keeping your marriage vows and commitments.

Taking Refuge requires the correct understanding of the good qualities of the Three Jewels as well as seriousness in keeping the Refuge precepts. They are the tool for you to use to undergo or bring about the positive changes in your actions, behavior, view, and thinking patterns.

The naïve hope of becoming instantly a good person, or of quickly gaining high realization, or for spontaneous positive change to occur in your life during the next overnight period is absolutely wrong and incorrect. You must not take Refuge with these hopes and expectations. It is better not to make yourself a bad Buddhist by mistaking or not knowing about the proper ways to go for Refuge. Instead it is much better to study Buddhism as much as you can with an open and unbiased mind. Make effort to be a good person and integrate Buddhist teachings into your everyday life, taking Refuge only when you are really ready—when you really know what Refuge means.

In short, you should take Refuge in the Three Jewels by understanding their unique natures and individual functions. **The function afforded by Refuge in the Buddha is spiritual guidance; the function of Refuge in the Dharma is practice; and the function of Refuge in the Sangha is spiritual support.** With these three aids you have all that is required to traverse the paths and bhumis and to obtain fortunate rebirth, full liberation from samsara, and a blissful omniscient mind.

You must not give up the Refuge in the Three Jewels once you have taken Refuge or divorce from them the way you might divorce from your spouses. Divorce is not the solution to the problem because the pain of divorce will remain in your mind or memory, and in addition you will not find any sense of comfort and security in your next marriage relationship.

Of course you will have full freedom to give up the Refuge. No person will punish you or stop you from doing it. However, having freedom to do so does not mean you should give it up or that there is no negative result from giving it up.

Your freedom to make the decision to give up the Refuge is not just a religious freedom; rather, it is also freedom within the religion. There is a natural negative in giving up the Three Jewels as your guide. It is like a throwing away your loving and compassionate parent who gives birth to you, who raises you with caring and love, who wishes you to be well and happy, who guides you in the wholesome way to live, who makes sure that you do not associate with bad influential friends, and who provides you all conducive factors for you education.

When you abandon the parent whose kindness cannot be repaid through any means, your act is by nature negative and this act will naturally have negative effects in your life. This negativity is not a punishment to you but it is an aftermath force, a natural consequence, of what you did.

CHAPTER EIGHT

Refuge Precepts to be Observed

How effective and meaningful taking Refuge and practicing Dharma are in your life solely depends on your proper observation of the Refuge precepts. Going for Refuge will be fruitless and meaningless if you don't live according the Refuge precepts and bring about positive change in your actions and behaviors. The power and the purpose of taking Refuge will be soon lost unless you mindfully observe the Refuge precepts.

The Refuge precepts are voluntary commitments from your heart to cultivate. After all, you took refuge in the Three Jewels in order to enjoy the fruits of the Refuge, to benefit from your practice. The precepts of Refuge are like your responsibility or commitment to give water to your plant, from the day you choose to take responsibility for this plant so that you can enjoy the fruit. The plant will not grow and bear fruit if you do not give it water regularly. To give water regularly is your commitment so as to ensure that the plant you planted will grow well and bear fruit.

Similarly, the Refuge precepts are your commitment to observe from the day you take Refuge. If you do not observe the Refuge precepts then the Refuge will not be meaningful and effective in your life and your Dharma practice. To observe the Refuge precepts mindfully in everyday life is your commitment. This allows the Refuge to be meaningful and to bear the fruit of an immense number of good qualities at the minimum level and the fruit of high spiritual realization at the maximum.

Once you have gone for Refuge you must live with the precepts of Refuge. In order to do this, you must know what the Refuge precepts are.

The precepts to be observed

There are two types of Refuge precepts, general and specific.

There are six general precepts:

You recall the good qualities of the Three Jewels, and you go for Refuge often in a day.

You recall the great kindness of the Three Jewels and do the food blessing with an intention to offer the first portion of your food and drink to the Three Jewels before consuming anything yourself.

You assist other living beings to establish themselves in a virtuous lifestyle with love and compassion.

You make supplication prayers to the Three Jewels before you attempt to engage in any activities either for your worldly or spiritual achievements.

You recall the benefits of Refuge, and you go for Refuge three times in the day and three times at night. You recall the kindness of the Buddha and the benefits of Refuge as you make three mindful prostrations upon waking up in the morning and three before retiring to bed at night.

In addition to observing these six general precepts you must put effort into making offerings before the sacred images of the Three Jewels. In general, there are seven types of offerings that you can make. They are: **clear water, scented water, fresh fruits, fresh flowers, fragrant incense, candle light and music.** The whole purpose of the offerings is their spiritual significance as an aid to your path practice. The offerings are discussed in detail in my book "*The Traditional Buddhist Altar.*"

It is extremely important that all the offering materials come from a wholesome source and by wholesome means. This means that they must not be obtained through stealing, lying or other subtle deceptive means. Rather they must be obtained through honest and sincere means.

When making offerings you must do so with a deep respect and in a humble way. You make the offerings in order to create merit to attain enlightenment for the benefit of all living beings. You must not think that you are doing some favor for the Three Jewels. You are making offerings as a essential part of your own Dharma practice in order to accelerate your progress on the path to enlightenment.

You can take Refuge in the Three Jewels three times in a day and three times at night by reciting the Refuge Formula. Before reciting the Refuge Formula you should bring the Three Jewels into your mind and recall their unique qualities. Then begin to recite this Refuge Formula with respect, trust and faith:

Lama La Kyab Su Chi Wo!
Sangay La Kyab Su Chi Wo!
Cho La Kyab Su Chi Wo!
Gen Dun La Kyab Su Chi Wo!! *(Repeat slowly 3 times)*

When you recite the Refuge Formula you must deeply hold the Three Jewels in your humble heart as

- The ultimate guide in this life and future lives
- The source of blessings
- The source of all paths to happiness
- The source of spiritual boons
- The root of joy and happiness
- The source of all beneficial teachings and practices

The specific precepts

The specific precepts are closely related to the functions of each of the Three Jewels. Since you have taken Refuge in the Buddha, you must respect all images of the enlightened beings and pay heartfelt homage whenever you view them. Always make effort to receive teachings from the living teachers who play the role of the Buddha.

Since you have taken Refuge in the Dharma, you must not do harm to any living being and you must make effort to help as much as you can. The essence of the Dharma is love, compassion, and caring for others. Respect all Dharma books and make sure not to leave them on the bare floor or in dishonorable places; do not carry them together with shoes or walk over them, or put them in places where they might be damaged. You must not engage in casual dispute or debate about the Dharma with non-Buddhist followers since this frequently turns into a fight, with hate, deep conflict and disharmony.

Since you have taken Refuge in the Sangha, you must pay respect to all ordained monks and nuns. You must not associate with people whose bad actions and bad habits are like a highly contagious disease. Also, you must not associate with those whose influence hinders your practice and disturbs your mind. The main aim of not associating with such people is to maintain solid, concentrated, and well directed practice.

In short, you must live observing the law of karma by cultivating what is taught to be practiced and abandoning what is taught to be abandoned concerning your activities of body, speech, and mind. You must cultivate the ten positive actions and avoid the ten negative actions. These will be discussed below in Chapter Ten and Chapter Eleven.

Your going for Refuge in the Three Jewels will be highly fruitful and effective in your life, not just at the spiritual level, but also in your everyday life. To live keeping these precepts and observing the law of karma will no doubt help you to reduce many unnecessary causes for your pain and sufferings and increase many of the causes for your joy, peace and happiness.

This is how going for Refuge protects you from what you don't desire and helps you to attain what you do desire.

However, taking Refuge in the Three Jewels and then not observing the Refuge precepts makes the Refuge completely meaningless, and its purpose is soon lost. This failure also causes the Buddhist and Buddha's teachings to have a negative image. It is similar to a bad student of an excellent teacher—the bad student gives the good teacher a bad name. The teacher's good qualities such as joy in teaching and setting a good example are disregarded and his or her reputation is ruined by the bad student's behavior and failure in learning because the student does no proper home work after school.

The benefits of going for Refuge

The benefits of going for Refuge are immeasurable. However, here are some of the benefits. This list might help you to see the critical meaning in taking Refuge.

> Refuge opens the door to all paths.
> It serves as the base for all vows and precepts.
> It increases merit and the force of virtue.
> It stops or closes the door to lower rebirth.
> It helps to avert the negative forces caused by humans or non-humans.
> It makes you worthy to uphold all lower and higher vows.
> It helps you to regard all living beings as precious and to treat them with respect.
> It makes you less greedy, less selfish, less arrogant, less malicious, and more forgiving to others' wrongdoing towards you and your loved ones.
> It helps you to be more prone to seek joy and happiness within and less expectant that you will be happy by obtaining material things.

- It helps you to make full preparation for your peaceful death and to obtain good rebirth.
- It makes you more ethical with a concern for others' well-being.
- It helps you to realize that this human life is your opportunity for attaining enlightenment and that you should not be a trouble maker on the earth.
- It makes you to realize the importance of extracting the essence of human life through practicing Dharma.
- It is the indispensable basis for empowerments of the secret Tantrayana.
- It is the key for opening the door of all types of Buddhist practice.
- It helps you to distance yourself from all negative actions and deeds so that your mind will not be invaded by evil thoughts.

The more you become humble before the three Jewels the more you are loved by others. The more you come under the care of the Three Jewels the more you become less critical of others, less fearful, and less hateful towards others' religion and beliefs.

Refuge creates an immense amount of merit—more than any other means—as stated in the *Immaculate Sutra*:

If all the merit of going for Refuge
Were to take a physical form,
The whole of space, entirely filled,
Would not be enough to contain it.

And similarly in the *Condensed Transcendent Wisdom*:

If the merit of going for Refuge took form,
All the three realms could never contain it.
Could the vast amount of water in all the great oceans
Ever be measured with a quarter-pint scoop?

After taking Refuge it is extremely important to devote yourself to your Dharma practice with a firm and irreversible interest and motivation. **As we said, the benefits of taking Refuge are immeasurable, but you must thoroughly know the unique spiritual qualities of each of the Three Jewels and their particular functions before taking Refuge.** In repeating what I said before—by placing strong emphasis on this point here again—I am trying to make sure you understand.

CHAPTER NINE

Karma

Over all the ultimate point of taking Refuge in the Three Jewels is to begin to live always observing the natural laws of karma. It is extremely difficult to prove the laws of karma merely by means of the force of logical reasoning. And even if a person would be extremely well versed and adept in logical reasoning, probably he could not even follow the process.

Therefore, meanwhile, you can observe the laws of karma by relying on the Buddha as a valid being with an omniscient mind that functions under the power of compassion and Bodhicitta. Your ability to rely on Buddha's words on karma comes from the power of Refuge through knowing the unique enlightened qualities of the Buddha.

Here are some quotations from the sutra which help you to know what the Buddha said about the laws of karma:

Moon and stars may fall to earth,
Mountains and valleys may crumble
And even the sky may vanish;
But you, O Buddha, speak nothing false.

From evil deeds comes suffering;
Therefore day and night
You should think and re-think
About how to avoid misery forever.

*The roots of all goodness lie
In the soil of appreciation for wholesomeness.
Constantly meditate upon how to ripen
The fruits that can grow therefrom.*

*O king, do not kill,
For all that live cherish life.
If you wish to live long and enjoy strong health yourself, respect life
And do not even think of killing.*

*Once you have committed an action, you will experience its concordant effects;
And you will not experience the effects of what you have not done.
Even in one hundred eons
Karma does not perish.
When the circumstances and the time arrive
You will surely feel its effect.*

*Do not scorn even the tiniest non-virtuous action,
Thinking that it will do no harm;
It is through the accumulation of drops of water
That a great vessel gradually fills.*

*Do not think that the cultivation
Of even a tiny virtue will not follow you.
Just as a large pot is filled
By falling drops of water,
So too are the steadfast filled up
By virtue accumulated a little at a time.*

*Once you have become certain that virtuous and nonvirtuous karma
Give rise to happiness and suffering in lives beyond,
Eradicate negative deeds and make effort to cultivate positive actions.
You who are without trust and power to understand it, do as you will.*

The great Indian Buddhist Teacher Acharya Vasubhandu has made a final conclusion about the Buddha's teachings on karma by saying:

*The complexity of the whole universe
Comes from the complexity of Karma.*

The complexity of karma should be very evident to your eyes. There is no satisfactory explanation other than karma for the formation of such an intricate and complex physical world and the complex experiences that living beings go through in every day of their lives.

The experiences arising during interaction with the external physical world, even when interacting with a single object, vary from being to being, from person to person. For instance, two people eat a piece of apple from the same half at the same time. One person finds its taste very satisfying but the other finds its taste very disgusting. The apple is not the one that makes these judgments, and the apple has no biased intention towards those two persons. However, the way the two people experience its taste is completely different; this difference is a fact and it cannot be refuted at all.

There is nothing wrong in the sense organs of the two persons and they are perfectly healthy. Also, the way a person experiences the taste of an apple is surely not determined by liking or disliking from their side. There must be something subtle determining the cause of the experiences of the two people to be so very different, so that they have totally opposite experiences of the apple's taste.

Similarly, two people or more live in a same house. One person finds the house conducive and happy, while a second person finds it inconducive and unhappy. A third person finds it neither conducive nor inconducive, and he is fine with the house. This vast difference in their life experiences has its own unique cause which you are not aware of.

Likewise, look at identical twins from the same biological parents who are raised in a healthy environment with love and affection, who receive the same education and guidance. Yet with this very similar upbringing:

One twin can be physically unattractive and the other can be attractive.

The one who is physically attractive can have a very troubled mind and behavior, and the one who is physically unattractive can have a very calm, gentle, caring and loving attitude and attractive behavior.

One twin becomes very successful in whatever he does, while the other always fails no matter what.

One has strong health and the other has frequent illnesses.

One is very generous and the other is very stingy.

One always attracts good friends and the other one repulses others.

One lives long and the other one's life is short.

One is always received and welcomed by others with respect and the other one is always treated by others with humiliating disrespect.

One acquires wealth more easily with less struggle and the other one always struggles and fails.

Similarly, one frequently become the victim of others' deception and lies even among his or her own friends and loved ones. The other one is well protected by his or her friends, employees, and even by strangers.

These differences are not just a matter of one being lucky and the other one being unlucky. Nor do these experiences occur by random coincidence, mere chance, or as a just punishment or reward meted out by higher beings. Nor are these experiences occurring without any cause.

Each of these experiences has its own unique cause that is the seed planted by one's own good or negative actions in past lives. The seeds that you planted in your past lives are described as karma in Buddhist teachings.

With regard to your action, any action performed through your body, speech or mind that is positive by nature and leads to joy and happiness is known as a good or positive action. Any action performed through your body, speech and mind that is harmful or negative by nature is identified as a negative action.

All sorts of good karma are created through the positive actions of body, speech and mind motivated by love, compassion and selflessness. All sorts of bad karma are created through the negative actions of body, speech and mind motivated by attachment, lust, anger, selfishness, greed, malice, jealousy, hatred and wrong view.

The good karmic seeds are solely responsible for the pleasant experiences in your life and for the formation of a soothing and pleasant physical environment in this life as well as your future lives. The bad karma alone are responsible for all sorts of unpleasant experiences and for the formation of a harsh and inconducive living environment in this life as well as your future lives.

How bright and happy a life you will have in your next rebirth is fully within your own present hands and effort. If you abandon the ten negative actions and cultivate the ten positive actions you will ensure that you will obtain a happy rebirth in a pleasant realm. If you fail to do this then you will roll down to an unhappy rebirth in one of the miserable realms without escape regardless of how cunning you are. **To live observing the laws of karma you must know the negative actions to be abandoned and the positive actions to be cultivated in everyday life.**

CHAPTER TEN

The Negative Actions to be Avoided

In general, there are many actions that are negative by nature. However, all types of negative actions can be grouped into ten. They are: **killing, stealing, sexual misconduct, lying, slander, harsh speech, idle gossip, covetousness, malicious thought and incorrect view.**

These actions are most apparently negative in the eyes of ordinary beings. However, there are more subtle negative actions that are closely related to each of the ten negative actions. For example, in the case of killing: influencing others to kill, taking joy or pleasure in killing, or having a sense of satisfaction over someone's death or murder. These acts are not so apparently negative for the ordinary mind. However, these acts are closely related to the actual act of killing and therefore they are negative by nature.

The same goes for killing any living being from a human to the smallest insect with a conscious choice. Killing by yourself, hiring someone to kill for you and instigating others to kill are the same because your intention is to kill.

Negative actions of body

The act of **killing** regardless of the victim is fully sufficient to create bad karma whose concordant result is sure and inevitable to occur with no escape in this or a future life.

The effects of the karma created through killing would be taking rebirth in a lower realm with an immense amount of pain and sufferings. Even if you are born again as a human you will still experience the effects of the law of karma: a short life, frequent illnesses, and either you or your loved ones being killed by others.

You will have a strong tendency to kill over and over. You will have a strong sense of pleasure in killing. Your environment will be harsh and unpleasant. The foods and drinks that you consume will have very little nutritional value and you will experience diseases of malnutrition.

Stealing is taking anything that is not given to you or not owned by you. There are several ways through which your act of stealing will be karmically completed.

Types of stealing are:

1. **Taking by force**. This means forceful seizure of others' possessions or property by a powerful individual, or by a small group like a gang, or by military force.
2. **Taking by stealth**. This means taking the belongings of others secretly, like a burglar, without being seen by the owner or anyone else.
3. **Taking by trickery**. This means taking the things of others in a business deal or in the process of a division of property. For instance, using a deceptive trick with weights and measures or other such subterfuges is taking by trickery.
4. **Borrowing money with no intention to pay back** is another way of stealing.
5. **Intentionally delaying returning things that you have borrowed, intending that the lender will forget about the loan or will give up hope of its return.** Using this subtle deceptive trick by endlessly delaying to pay back the person from whom you borrowed money, books, etc. is another way of stealing.

Through these various ways of stealing you create negative karma. The unavoidable and inevitable effects of the karma from stealing would be taking rebirth in a lower realm with a immense amount of pain and sufferings. Even if you are born as a human you will still experience effects such as a lack of material necessites, living with the constant threat of not having enough for your survival, and being yourself frequently the victim of random theft.

You will have a strong tendency to steal over and over. You will have a strong sense of taking joy over stealing. Your environment will be dangerous with thieves and robbers. The place where you live will be threatened by drought and famine, and the trees will bear no fruit. Your external environment will lack natural beauty and your enjoyment will be very limited in the place where you are forced to live.

Sexual misconduct primarily refers to having sexual intercourse with a person who is married or engaged to someone else; or with a person who is suitable but for whom it is the wrong time such as during menstruation or recovery from child birth; or during illness and distress in which the intercourse is painful and leads to a mental or physical problem. Sexual intercourse with a person who is under age or who is a child is a serious immoral act of sexual abuse. It has very heavy karmic effects as it is more than the misconduct of sexual activity.

The majority of divorces in the world are primarily caused by sexual misconduct, or because of a sexual relationship without love, care, and respect from both sides or a sexual relationship where people try to take unfair advantage of each other.

In addition, many divorces in the West are caused by too much sexual freedom. Many people confuse sexual freedom and sexual misconduct. They engage in sexual misconduct confusing it with sexual freedom and they do not see the negativities of their actions. In the West, there is an urgent need for educating people about what is sexual freedom versus what is sexual misconduct in order to stop much pain and suffering both within families and at the social level.

The gravest sexual misconduct is having an affair with a married man or woman. This act causes a great deal of pain, disharmony, distrust, conflict, bloody fighting and bitter divorce, and it puts the children into the midst of confusion and fear. Sexual misconduct causes unforgettably painful memories that last for a whole lifetime.

There is a Tibetan saying: *The bad memory remains on the earth even when the body dissolves into the earth after death.* You must not do any negative thing that results in what this Tibetan saying predicts!

The unavoidable and inevitable effects of the karma created through sexual misconduct are: you will take lower rebirth in the miserable realm. You will meet with a spouse who is not only unattractive but who also behaves in a very loose or hostile manner. The relationship will be very disharmonious and there will be much conflict, argument, fighting, and constant blame thrown on each other's character.

In brief, you will always meet with someone who is untrustworthy, contentious, disloyal, abusive, extremely jealous, very controlling, and intentionally causing arguments and fights. You cannot escape from meeting with such a partner until the karma created from the sexual misconduct is fully exhausted, after you have experienced its full effects.

There are more effects of the karma created through sexual misconduct. You will have a strong tendency to indulge in sexual misconduct in your next life. You will have extreme difficulty in keeping your wife or husband, and you will suffer from losing your spouse over and again.

You will be born in a place where there is no natural beauty—a place filled with disgusting substances that make your life very uncomfortable and limit enjoyable activities.

Negative actions of speech

Lying is the act of telling an untruth through changing your apparent perception and with the intention to deceive others for your personal interest. There are different ways by which you lie: words, physical gestures, choosing to say something other than what you know to be a fact, falsifying, or concealing.

Among the lies, lying about the attainment of superhuman qualities or higher spiritual realization is the gravest, for example: saying that you have clairvoyance or some psychic power to see others' future and to read others' minds, etc. although you don't.

The inevitable effects of the karma created through lying are: you will take lower rebirth in the miserable realm beyond your control and will experience an immense amount of pain and suffering with no outside help. Even if you are reborn as a human you not only will often be criticized and belittled, but also you will frequently be lied to by others—including your own loved ones.

Often you will be falsely accused and blamed by others and you will have no support or witness to protect you. You will frequently become the victim of others' lies. You will have a strong impulse to lie over and over without any reason or purpose. You will find false enjoyment in lying and watching how others get confused and become perplexed by your false words.

You will not succeed in any task that you do. Your friends and employees will be deceitful, and you will be very fearful and have many causes to be afraid.

Slander is an act of intentionally causing division and conflict among families, friends, congregations, and married couples, etc. through your words. You slander either out of jealousy or hatred. There are two types of slander. The first is saying something negative with a wish to cause disharmony between those who are already in harmony. The second is saying something with a wish to prevent harmony between those who are in disharmony.

The gravest instance of slander in causing division and disharmony is causing a rupture in the spiritual community, between teacher and disciples, or in the circle of spiritual brothers and sisters.

The inevitable negative effects of the karma created through the act of slander are: you will take unfortunate rebirth in the lower realm and will experience immense sufferings with no outside help. Even if you are born as a human, you will often lose friends, and your family members and employees will not get along and will misbehave; they will create many hindrances so that it is hard for you to succeed in whatever you wish to accomplish.

You will have a strong impulse from your birth to indulge in slander. You will find a false pleasure in slandering and you will take joy in others' disharmony. You will be forced to live in a place that is bumpy, craggy, uneven, and difficult to traverse, and you will have many causes to be afraid.

Harsh or abusive speech is an act of using unpleasant words with the intention to cause emotional pain and disturbance. Your harsh statement may be true or untrue— but as long as it has the potential to create emotional pain, it is included as harsh speech.

For instance, a person has the habit of eating like a pig, making noises such as *chak-chak*, the way the pig does when it eats. If you say to that person disparagingly "you eat like a pig," although what you say is somewhat true and he does have that habit, still your speech is going to be painful for his mind and therefore it is none other than harsh speech.

The inevitable negative effects of the karma created through the act of harsh or abusive speech are: you will take lower rebirth in the unpleasant realm and will experience immense suffering with no external help. You will always hear unpleasant words about yourself and quarrelsome speech. You will meet with an abusive boss at your work and you will find it difficult to escape from the abusiveness.

You will have a strong tendency to indulge in harsh speech due your past habituation. You will find a false pleasure in this act and take joy over how others are affected by your harsh speech. This will put you in a vicious cycle, making the problem deeper and deeper in each of your lifetimes.

You will be forced to live in a place that is full of thorns, bushes, sharp stones, poisonous plants and grasses, and many dangerous animals. The place lacks natural beauty and you will have no external things to enjoy. Everything you have in that place only causes you to be afraid.

Idle chatter is an act of talking a lot without any meaning and purpose except that of messing up your mind and others' minds by expressing thoughts and emotions of anger, hatred, attachment, jealousy, lust, fantasy, greed, fear—all sorts of negative stimulation.

Examples of idle chatter are: talking about sex, prostitution, war, rumor, the pleasure of drugs and alcohol, or the pleasure of "messing around" with men and women; bragging about one's own perfections and belittling others, concealing one's wrong doing or blaming it on others, as well as talking about things with an intention to cause damage to others' name and reputation by means of making up baseless stories. When there is nothing to talk about that has positive meaning and purpose then it is best to maintain a noble silence.

The inevitable negative effects of the karma created through the act of idle chattering are: you will take lower rebirth in the unpleasant realm and will experience an immense amount of suffering.

Even if you are born as a human still you will experience many negative effects of the karma. Your words will carry very little meaning and will serve no purpose. Others will treat your words with disrespect and put no value at all on what you say. Others will make insulting comments about your words. Your words will be very unclear and cause lots of misunderstandings that will give rise to conflict. You will have no self confidence in whatever you attempt to do.

You will have a strong impulse to indulge in idle gossip in your next life. You will find a false joy in idle chatter and this will put into motion a vicious cycle. You will be forced to live in a place where fruit trees do not bear fruit or where they bear fruit at the wrong time, and even if they do bear fruit it will not ripen on time; even if it ripens on time still it cannot have a good taste or be nutritious. The place in which you live will lack many external comforts such as parks, groves, rivers, lakes, mountains, valleys, evergreen trees, fragrant vegetation and flowers, etc.

Negative actions of mind

Covetousness is a desirous or acquisitive thought towards others' property; you want it to be yours and owned by you. Covetousness is mixed with jealousy and an attachment that goes beyond the boundary of your own possessions, so you become attached to others' belongings and spouses. Because of covetousness you attempt to possess others' belongings and spouses, inventing schemes to get hold of them, etc.

The inevitable negative effects of the karma created through the act of covetousness are: you will take lower rebirth in the miserable realm right after death and will experience much pain and sufferings, all of which suffering seems very unfair to you.

Even if you are born as a human, still you will experience many of the karmic effects of covetousness. You will have very strong attachment and no sense of contentment with whatever you possess. Your mind will be controlled by attachment and this will create deep feelings of insecurity with regard to your relationships, material wealth, social status, etc.

You will be forced to live in a place where the natural resources diminish year by year. Nothing will increase and flourish due to drought, famine, a lack of natural nourishment in the soil, and harsh elemental disharmony.

Ill will or malicious thought is a mental act of wishing for others to suffer or wishing them harm, and brooding with anger, hatred, and jealousy. You feel happy upon seeing others' pain and feel unhappy upon seeing others' joy. These are included in the negative action ill will.

When you harbor or hold on to this feeling you create karma within the mental level and there is no need of any external action in order to create karma in the case of ill will.

The inevitable negative effects of the karma created through the act of ill will are: you will take lower rebirth in the unhappy realm and will experience much pain and suffering.

Even if you are born as a human, still you will experience the many negative effects of ill will. Your mind will be controlled by anger, hatred and jealousy. You will have a very troubled mind, and a troubled mind is a great cause of unhappiness.

You will not seek things to benefit you and help solve your problem. Instead you will have a tendency to seek destructive things that make your problem worse, such as alcohol and drugs and relying on them as a remedy for your unhappiness.

You will be forced to live in a place where there are epidemics, infectious illnesses, constant quarrels and disputes, torture, rape, and bloody fights. You can notice these in many parts of the world in which we live.

These problems continue from generation to generation, decade to decade and century to century with no help from the rest of the world. The reason is that on one hand the rest of the world has no compassion and also thinks that there is no self gain from helping. On the other hand, the negative effects of the karmic seeds planted in former lives by those living in that area are unavoidable by any outside means.

Wrong view or incorrect view is a mistaken view or belief with regard to the truth of reality. There are four main types of wrong views.

1. The willful denial of the existence of the natural law of karma. It is a wrong belief that intentional actions have no karmic effect, and thinking that things occur in your life randomly, or as a force of evil, or as a reward or punishment from God.

2. The view that there are a permanent self/soul and an eternally existing creator of the universe, such as God. It is a belief that everything in this world whether pleasant or unpleasant, good or bad, joyful or sad, rich or poor, strong or weak, successful or failed, pretty or ugly, lucky or unlucky, smart or stupid, etc. is created by God or just occurs spontaneously without its corresponding pre-existing causes and conditions.

3. The view of nihilism. It is the wrong belief that all things just occur by themselves and that there are no past and future lives, no karma, and no possibility for humans to attain high spiritual realization through training and practice.

4. The view that one's own religion is supreme, best and right, and that all others are wrong and false. The present Pope, Benedict XVI, has said: *"Jesus came on earth to build only one church [that is referring to the Catholic church], and all others are either wrong or false."* This is nothing other than "wrong view" and it has tremendous potential to create disharmony, conflict, fighting, hatred, anger, resentment, killing and intolerance. This wrong view acts as a poison in the human world.

You create a heavy karma through holding these wrong views. The inevitable negative effects of the karma created through wrong view are: you will take lower rebirth in the darkest realm with intense pain and sufferings. Even if you are reborn as a human your mind will be controlled by deep confusion. You will experience stupidity; you will lack both knowledge and wisdom.

You will be the victim of wrong or misleading teachings and information. You will have bad views and will be extremely deceitful. You will have a serious learning problem, and whatever you learn will easily be dissipated or forgotten. You will be in an environment where there are very many causes for misunderstanding, confusion and fear, with misleading teachers, misleading friends, and a lack of supportive community.

These are the **ten negative actions** through which you create bad karma. The completion of each of these actions automatically leaves an imprint on your mind-stream like a permanent bad credit record. This imprint remains intact through eons and it never perishes until it brings its effect. The karmic seed will bring its effect when it meets with the right conditions and the right time, and whoever has created that karma will surely experience the effect without escape.

Through clearly knowing about the natural relationship between the volitional act and its unavoidable karmic effect, you must make effort not to indulge in any of the ten negative actions. Mindfully abstaining from the negative actions is the best way to take care of yourself. Also, it is the true way to show love, compassion, and respect to yourself.

You must make effort at all times to avoid the slightest wrongdoings, and to apply yourself to do whatever positive deeds you can, no matter how insignificant they may seem. As long as you are not making that effort, each instance of negative action is leading you into many kalpas of life in the miserable realms.

Never underestimate the minutest wrong deed, thinking that it cannot do that much harm. As the great Indian Buddhist master Shantideva says:

If the negative deed of an instant
Can lead to a Kalpa in the hell of ultimate Torment,
Then with all the evil of samsara's time without beginning,
What chance is there of going to higher realms?

Similarly in the *Sutra of the Wise and the Foolish* you find:

Do not take lightly small misdeeds,
Believing they can do no harm.
Even a tiny spark of fire
Can set alight a mountain of hay.

It is extremely important not to do any negative deeds. However, whenever you do commit misdeeds, due to lack of mindfulness, you must not leave them without purifying them—immediately if possible, without putting off until the next day, because the seed of every single negative action greatly multiplies over time.

Purification of negative deeds

Purification is a process—in the first place—of making the negative karmic seeds left behind by the force of negative actions stop increasing. Then in the middle, purification makes them weak. Finally it makes them totally to lose their potency so that they cannot ever bear their negative effects.

The purification practice requires the strong support of four powers. In the absence of the four powers purification practice will not work. The four powers are:

The power of support
The power of regret
The power of resolution
The actual antidotal power

The **power of support** is provided by taking refuge in Vajrasattva and generating a pure intention such as love, compassion, and bodhicitta. Also, the power of support can be provided by the object to which you address your confession.

The **power of regret** comes from the feeling of **shame** of doing negative deeds and the feeling of **fear** of their unavoidable negative karmic consequences. To have a strong feeling of regret requires sincerity and honesty in acknowledging your negative actions as totally wrong without holding any sense of external reason to justify your actions.

The **power of resolution** is a firm commitment never to commit them again from today, even at the cost of your life. In the *Sutra in Three Parts* we say:

I vow to stop from now on.

Similarly the *Prayer of Sukhavati* says:

Without resolve for the future there is no purification,
So I vow from today on never to commit negative actions,
Even if it costs me my life.

Your resolution cannot be firm and strong if you don't have a powerful feeling of regret that gives you goose bumps. Therefore, to have a sincere and strong feeling of regret is most essential in the practice of purification.

The actual **antidotal power** can be accomplished through various virtuous deeds and mantra recitations, such as **reading holy sutras, making prostrations, building temples and stupas, reciting the holy names of the thirty-five confession Buddhas, reciting the hundred seed syllable purification mantra of Vajrasattva, etc.**

Among the various forms of using the antidotal power, the recitation of the hundred seed syllable mantra of Vajrasattva is the most effective and powerful.

This practice can be done with a clear visualization of Vajrasattva in front of you or on the crown of your head, maintaining the force of the feeling of regret in your heart, and reciting the hundred seed syllable mantra as many times as you can with a good degree of mindfulness.

While making sure not to commit any negative actions and doing the purification practice daily, you should make effort to do positive or wholesome deeds as much as you can with your conscious effort. When you do this then the observation of Refuge precepts will be fully completed.

CHAPTER ELEVEN

The Positive Deeds to be Cultivated

A positive action is any action that necessarily leads to joy and happiness as its sole result without the possibility that there will be anything else for its result other than joy and happiness.

There are many different types of actions that can be positive by their nature. All forms of positive action comprise the resolute vow never to commit the corresponding negative action described in Chapter Eleven. For example, when you generously give you are vowing never to commit the negative action of not giving from that instant moment.

All possible positive actions can be grouped into ten:

Not only abandoning killing but also actively saving and protecting lives
Not only abandoning stealing but also actively giving and sharing
Not only abandoning sexual misconduct but also actively respecting and honoring the other person in your healthy relationship
Not only giving up lying but also actively telling the truth and being honest
Not only giving up slander but also actively speaking with harmonious words
Not only giving up harsh and insulting speech but also actively speaking soft, gentle, pleasing, and loving words
Not only giving up idle chatter but also actively maintaining a noble silence if talk is not necessary or useful

Not only abandoning covetousness but also actively practicing rejoicing and having a sense of contentment with what you have

Not only abandoning malicious thoughts but also actively cultivating love and a benevolent intention

Not only abandoning wrong view but also actively being open, unbiased and receptive, and relying on correct logical reasoning for finding the truth

Positive actions of body

Not killing but saving and protecting lives is by nature a virtuous deed and it bears many desirable effects. The act of saving and protecting lives includes doing things that improve the quality of life—for example, providing material resources for clean drinking water in order to prevent the various illnesses caused by waterborne pathogens in many third world countries. Your act of purifying drinking water prolongs life, stop illnesses and builds good health. Similarly, it is a virtuous deed to provide highly nutritious food and drink in order to prevent malnutrition in different parts of the world.

Likewise, it is virtuous to use your resources to build schools, children's hospitals or maternity clinics as places where people can get various kinds of help—cure for sickness, education, ethical guidelines, protection for mother and baby from many possible complications of pregnancy and childbirth. Through such positive deeds you create wholesome karma. This is your real wealth. It is the unfailing cause for your future happiness and happy rebirth.

The inevitable positive effects of this karma are: you will take high rebirth in the happy realm. You will have strong health and you will not experience much illness. You will have a long and happy life. You will have an attractive physical appearance. You will be loved and cherished by others. You will never see any of your loved ones and friends being killed. You will not be subject to be killed by others for any reason, in any conditions.

You will have an innate feeling of love and compassion towards all living beings. You will cherish all forms of life and you will be in a position to help all according to both their temporary and ultimate needs. Your actions and behavior will never become a threat to others. Others will always find a sense of comfort, security and protection in your presence.

The place where you live will be filled with natural beauty. It will be free of life threatening diseases. The food and drink will have a high nutritional value, and no food or drink will cause digestive problems. Your means to find enjoyment in that place will have no limits or restrictions from any outside conditions.

Not stealing but giving and sharing is a positive deed by nature and it results in many desirable effects which can reach many living beings. The act of giving and sharing your resources with others unties the knots of miserliness in your heart and helps you to be generous and not to be attached to your possessions.

Attachment to your possessions only gives rise to fear, suspicion, greed, and a feeling of being threatened—these feelings are your own taskmaster that turns you permanently into a slave. Giving and sharing will bring you a sense of joy and satisfaction as their natural reward. Your resources will become greatly helpful to many living beings and your generosity creates the karmic cause for you to obtain vast material wealth in your future life.

If you don't engage in giving and sharing your resources in a wise and proper way while they are under your control, then one day they will go to waste in someone else's hands, over which you don't have any control. You must make sure that this will not happen to you and your resources. The only way to do this is to practice giving and sharing with others with a good intention and using your resources to support education, medicine, religion, orphanage, children's hospital, homeless shelter, etc. These good deeds of giving and sharing your resources with a positive intention will surely create good karmic credit and will bear many desirable results in your future lives.

The inevitable results of the karma created through the positive deeds of giving and sharing your resources are: you will take higher rebirth in the pleasant and comfortable realm. You will have an abundance of material wealth. You will have great success in whatever you wish to accomplish with a small effort and without struggle. Your karma gives you a magnetic force that is like pollen on a flower so that you will naturally attract good things towards you just as pollen attracts bees.

Not only you will have maximum enjoyment of your material wealth, but your material wealth will not deteriorate due to outside conditions. You will be in the best position to practice generosity and this will continuously help to increase your wealth and bring you joy and satisfaction as its natural reward.

You will find joy and pleasure in the act of giving, and you will be happy to see how others are benefited by your help. The place where you live will be filled with medicinal plants, fruit trees, fragrant flowers and high-yielding crops, and all foods and drinks will be highly nutritious.

Not only avoiding sexual misconduct but responsibly respecting and honoring others' relationships is an act that is wholesome in its very nature and it gives rise to many good results. Sexual activity must be based on love, ethics and healthy responsibility. Sexual activity must not become a cause for pain and suffering to anyone. Sexual activity should be a mere expression of love, caring and nourishment for the male and female's healthy relationship.

The definite good results of the karma created from the moral act of avoiding sexual misconduct are: you will take higher rebirth in the clean and attractive realms. You will meet a spouse who is attractive, loving, caring, loyal, truthful, respectful, kind and pleasing. You will experience a very harmonious relationship. Your relationship will be secured and protected by your mutual trust, respect and love. You will find real meaning and purpose in the relationship, and you will be happy and content with your spouse.

Others will admire and respect your relationship. Your healthy and morally based relationship will serve as a good example to others. Your children will be happy and they will find value in ethics, true love, respect, trust and loyalty. Your children will be nurtured and will grow up valuing the basic goodness of heart and mind.

It is obvious that many divorced parents' children are more unhappy, have more behavioral trouble, are more confused, have unsteady mood, are more distanced from both parents, are more unsettled with a weak focus on their studies, and are slow to learn at school. These problems of the children follow on the problems of selfish and troubled parents.

Positive actions of speech

Not only avoiding lying but also being truthful is an act that is good by nature. The karma created through this act will bear many positive effects, such as: you will take high rebirth in the conducive realm. You will have a very soothing and pleasing voice. Your words will be naturally truthful and highly regarded by others. Your words will be very subduing and dignifying.

Others will hold you as a truthful witness. Your words will be well obeyed and respected by others. You will never become a victim of others' random lies. You will not be blamed by others for their own wrongdoings. You will never—in all time and space—be deceived by others.

The place where you live will have many causes and conditions for you to be highly successful in whatever you do. The place will be harmonious, with no external threats to your well-being and success. The place will be filled with natural beauty.

Not only avoiding slander but also actively practicing and speaking harmonious words is an act that is wholesome by nature. The karma created through this act will bear many desirable results, such as that you will take fortunate rebirth in a happy realm. You will have a very pleasing and comforting voice. Your speech will naturally lead to harmony and will never cause conflict or dispute. Rather, your words will resolve conflicts and disputes.

You will become the most helpful counselor for others who seek direction. You will become an indisputably good judge in all worldly conflicts and disputes. You will not hear any unpleasant words about yourself from others. You will be worthy of praise and respect.

Not only avoiding harsh and insulting speech but actively practicing soft, pleasant and pleasing words is an act that is virtuous by nature. This act will provide comfort, joy, inspiration and an uplifted feeling in the minds of others. Your pleasing words become jewelry to the others' golden ears. The proper practice of using soft and pleasing words naturally creates a good karma.

The karma created through this act never fails to bring many wanted results such as: you will take higher rebirth in the happy realm. You will always hear pleasant and complimentary words from others about yourself. You will have an elegant speech that induces joy in the minds of others. Your words will have high potential to make a positive difference in others' lives, and your words will not cause any confusion or misunderstanding. You will have a respectful circle of friends and workers who never put you down or bring shame on you.

The place where you live will have great natural beauty. There will be a waterfall where it is needed. There will be a lake and a pond where they are needed. There will be trees and flowers where they are needed. There will be a meadow where it is needed. There will be a mountain where it is needed. There will be a river where it is needed. There will be parks and gardens where they are needed for your comfort and enjoyment.

Not only avoiding idle chatter but also actively maintaining a noble silence when talk is not necessary is an act that is wholesome in its very nature. This positive action helps to prevent many unnecessary conflicts and problems, and much distrust. Maintaining a noble silence when talk is not necessary or not helpful is far more useful than energy-draining idle chattering. There is a sense of joy and comfort in noble silence. This act of maintaining a noble silence when talk is neither helpful nor necessary creates a good karma.

The karma created through this act will bring many positive effects beyond our ordinary minds' comprehension, such as: you will take fortunate rebirth in the happy realm. You will have a calm and peaceful mind that enables you to pay strong attention. Your words will carry weight to have strong positive impact on others. Your words will be cherished by others with respect. Others will not criticize, belittle or make fun of your words.

The place where you live will be a fertile land which produces an immense crop of whatever you grow and cultivate. The seasons are timely and predictable.

Positive actions of mind

Not only abandoning covetousness but also actively cultivating a sense of rejoicing in others' good fortune is an act that is wholesome in its very nature. It helps to bring joy and a sense of pleasure in others' happiness and material wealth, etc. It acts as an antidote to jealousy.

You yourself will be benefited by others' happiness and wealth. This act of cultivating rejoicing and pleasure at the good fortune of others creates a good karma.

The karma created through this act will bear many desirable effects such as, you will take high rebirth in the conducive realm. Your wishes will be easily fulfilled and you will be happy and contented with what you have.

You will not experience strong attachment and thereby you will have a peaceful mind. Your possessions will be well protected without external threats and harms. You will be easy to please by even a small gift and you will find a meaning in the gift that will make you happy and thankful towards whomever it comes from.

The place where you live will have good seasonal harvests. Your happiness and material prosperity will easily increase from year to year, and there will be many conducive conditions available so that you will succeed in whatever you attempt to accomplish.

Not only abandoning malicious thoughts and feelings but also actively practicing love, compassion, a sense of closeness and a wish for all others to be happy is an act that is wholesome by nature. It acts as an antidote to anger, hatred and resentment. The proper cultivation of the wish for others to be happy with a firm commitment not to harbor ill will creates good karma.

The karma created through this act will bear many desirable effects such as, you will take high rebirth in the happy realm. You will have a kind, gentle, loving and caring mind. Your mind will not be subject to self-inflicted pain and it will not be obscured by delusions. You will have a joyful wish to make others happy. You will have special skill and power to provide mental, emotional

The Positive Deeds to be Cultivated

and psychological comfort to others. Even if you are not a healer, nor a trained doctor, nor a realized person, still you will have those healing qualities in you naturally without training and learning.

The place where you live will be free from many life threatening causes and conditions such as widespread epidemics, infectious illnesses, wrong teachings, disputes and quarrels, poisonous creatures and plants, filth and bad odor, etc. You will experience a very comfortable and protected life.

Not only abandoning wrong view but also actively cultivating an open and rational mind is an act that is positive by nature. This mind helps you to have a healthy access in your search for the truth, and your human intelligence is not disabled by the force of blind faith rooted in baseless fear.

The proper cultivation of an open and rational mind creates a healthy karma. The karma created through this act will bear many positive effects such as, you will take high rebirth in the very conducive realm where there are no wrong and misleading teachings, teachers or information. You will always meet with a loving and compassionate teacher who will lead you to the correct path to joy and happiness.

You will have an innate learning capability which will lead to vast and profound knowledge and wisdom. You will be free from confusion and fear. You will have a clear mind with a high power to discern between right and wrong, truth and falsehood.

The place where you live will have all necessary conditions for the growth of goodness. The external environment will be clean and enjoyable, and it will have all the means for protection from any danger or threat.

The action of karma in general

All the precepts of Refuge are included in practicing the ten positive actions and abandoning the ten negative actions. When you live observing the natural laws of what is good to be cultivated and what is bad to be avoided, then you are protected from pain and suffering and gifted with joy and happiness. This is what is known as Refuge.

The good and bad things that you have done in this life are your only possession when you die, and the good and bad karmic records will naturally follow you even after death, just as the shadow of your own body follows you wherever you go on a sunny day. Whatever strength, power, wealth, friends, loved ones, family members, name and reputation or high social status you may now enjoy— none of it follows you when you die.

The good karma created through practicing the ten positive actions and abandoning the ten negative actions with a firm determination and conscious effort will surely follow you into the next life. This good karma propels you into higher rebirth in the happy realm. The bad karma created through practicing the ten negative actions propels you into lower rebirth in the miserable realm.

The *Sutra of Instructions to the King* says:

When the moment comes to depart, O king,
Neither possessions, power, friends nor family can follow.
But wherever beings come from, wherever they go,
Their actions follow them like their own shadow.

All the effects of the good karma and bad karma may not be immediately evident and identifiable, but they definitely do not just fade away. When the right conditions come together one day, you will experience the effects of each and every good and bad karmic seed you have planted during your lifetimes:

Even after a hundred eons
Beings' karmic imprints never perish.
When the right conditions come together
Their effect will surely and fully ripen.

The tiniest karmic seed can give rise to unimaginable results—like the seed of the Bodhi tree which gives rise to a huge tree which has thousands of branches and which produces millions of leaves every year.

The growth of the karmic fruits actually cannot be minutely described and estimated. Therefore, it is important not to omit doing even small or minor positive deeds in every moment. For instance, a fly may be struggling and drowning in your swimming pool water. When you notice it you may ignore it and never think what you could do to save its life, since saving the life of a fly seems to you a very small or minor good deed. However, when it comes to the laws of karma, saving the fly's life is not an insignificant good deed. Making conscious effort to free the fly from drowning in the water creates a karmic seed that will produce inestimable good results in the future. This is why the *Sutra of the Wise and the Foolish* says:

Do not take lightly small good deeds,
Believing they can hardly help:
For drops of water one by one
In time can fill a giant pot.

The Positive Deeds to be Cultivated

Likewise, the *Treasury of Precious Qualities* says:

From seeds no bigger than a mustard grain
Grow vast Ashota trees, which in a single year
Can put out branches each a league in length.
But even greater is the growth of good and evil.

Whatever you experience as good or bad is the effect of what you did in the past. What you do today, good or bad, is the cause for whatever you will experience in the future. When you do good it is like planting a medicinal seed in the field of your mind. The continuity of your mind can never be broken. Similarly, when you do a bad deed it is like a planting a poisonous seed in the field of your mind.

If the seed is medicinal, the sprout, trunk, branches, leaves, buds, flowers and fruits will be medicinal and beneficial, and they cannot possibly be poisonous; this is natural and according to the law of cause and effect. If the seed is poisonous, the sprout, trunk, branches, leaves, buds, flowers and fruits will be poisonous and cannot possibly be medicinal; this too is according to natural causal law.

It is clearly said in the *Treasury of Precious Qualities*:

If the root is medicinal, so are the shoots.
If it is poisonous, must the shoots not be the same?
What makes an act positive or negative is not how it looks
Or its size, but the good or bad intention behind it.

Though it seems to you that your effort to save the fly from drowning is minor or childish, in fact the deed is not at all childish—due to the force of your positive intention, whether the intention is based on love, compassion, or a feeling of how the poor fly is struggling in the midst of fear, panic, destitution, helplessness and not knowing what to do. When you make the conscious effort to release the fly from drowning, not only do you save its life but you also free this other sentient being from fear, panic, destitution and a feeling of helplessness.

It is important always to make effort to save the lives of any form of living creatures, whether big, small, harmful or harmless, poisonous or non-poisonous; flies or ants, worms or termites, mice or cockroaches, spiders, etc. Whenever you find them in your house or in your room, try not to get rid of them by killing, but rather attempt to get rid of them harmlessly by releasing them into nature wherever they go and live. Getting rid of them by killing is easy but the natural negative effects of killing are heavy and not easy to escape.

Similarly, you must make every possible effort to do virtuous deeds regardless of whether the deeds seem very minor or not. The tiniest virtuous deeds can sow great virtuous seeds that bear inestimable positive results.

In conclusion: every negative karmic seed will multiply over time if it is not purified and if the purification is not supported by regret, resolve and the actual antidotal application. Similarly, every positive karmic seed and virtue will increase if you dedicate it selflessly for the benefit of all sentient beings. Take for example the positive karma and virtuous seed created through the good deed of abstaining from killing with your conscious effort even when you are in a situation where one might usually kill. Dedicating this virtuous deed for the cause of all living being to live long, to enjoy good health free from illnesses, and ultimately to attain enlightenment is meritorious and will bear positive fruit.

Daily practice after taking Refuge

When you have taken Refuge in the Three Jewels, you must do at least one brief mindful practice each night before retiring to bed. The following is a brief mindful practice that you can do:

Stage one: From your respectful and humble heart, make three prostrations before the inspiring image of the compassionate teacher Shakyamuni Buddha.

Stage two: Sit comfortably on your cushion or chair. Deeply reflect on the impermanence of life and motivate yourself to do good, with a firm determination to avoid doing evil.

Stage three: Generate sincerely the feeling of love and compassion by making the uncontrived wish for all living beings to be happy and for all beings to be free from pain and suffering, just as you wish these for yourself.

Stage four: Reflect on what you have done during the day between waking up in the morning and now. Whatever you find of bad things that you have done mindlessly, you should see them as a poison that you have consumed and that is now in your system and which sooner or later is bound to create pain and suffering. This will help you to generate a strong feeling of regret with a sense of urgency to get rid of the poison from your system.

Stage five : Based on the feeling of regret towards the negative actions that you have committed during that day, you do purification by reciting the Vajrasattva mantra with trust in the purifying power of the mantra while your mind is under the influence of regret. The Vajrasattva mantra:

OM VAJRA SATTVA HUNG PHED (recite 3, 7 or 21 times)

Stage six: Make a firm commitment not to repeat any similar negative action from today. You make this commitment before the eyes of Vajrasattva or your root guru as your witness.

Stage seven: Reflect on what good things you have done during this day. Feel joyful and take a sense of satisfaction in your good deeds. Dedicate your good deeds for the higher cause—the benefit of all sentient beings—without holding the good deeds in your personal possession for your selfish interest.

Stage eight: Then go to bed in a peaceful and virtuous state of mind. Think that your head is now peacefully resting in the compassionate lap of the Buddha who never fails to protect you when you fulfill your responsibility which is to live observing the natural laws of karma.

CHAPTER TWELVE

To Become a Buddhist Through Taking the Refuge Ordination

To be a Buddhist means to place emphasis on cultivating the inner mental and spiritual causes for peace and happiness rather than relying on principles based on belief in a divine being or on a theory of creation. Therefore, a Buddhist is one who seeks happiness within and who sees that external things and objects are incapable of bringing true happiness, and are only useful for momentary pleasure or comfort which soon turn into the pain of dissatisfaction and frustration.

True Buddhist practice begins with taking Refuge from the depths of your heart in the Three Jewels—Buddha, Dharma and Sangha—as the sole spiritual guide on your journey on the path to enlightenment for the benefit of all living beings bound to live in the water, under and on the earth, and in the air and space.

The speed of your spiritual progress can be very fast due to

1. the force of your reliance on the guidance of the Buddha
2. integrating the Dharma as part of your daily life
3. looking up to the exalted qualities of the Sangha to inspire your determination to acquire those qualities for yourself through vigorous practice—not by merely wishing or having faith.

Taking Refuge is essential

This is why taking Refuge is essential for you:

> To be serious in learning and practicing the Dharma
> To be serious in bringing positive changes in your life
> To be serious in attaining enlightenment with an altruistic intention to provide permanent freedom for all living beings from the terrors of samsara

There is no better or greater person than one who selflessly works for the well-being of everyone without exception through love and compassion.

Refuge is the one thing that helps you to become a warmhearted person, and makes what you do meaningful and beneficial to yourself as well as others, either directly or indirectly.

For this reason, the day of the full moon is a golden opportunity to conduct the Refuge ordination ceremony. The full moon acts as a stimulating force to make your energy channels more active and receptive.

Nature and structure of the actual ceremony

Preliminary preparation where the ceremony is to be held

1. An inspiring image of Buddha Shakyamuni that has been blessed and consecrated must be placed where the ceremony is going to be held.
2. In front of this image of the Buddha, attractive material offerings must be arranged, such as: **clear water, scented water, candle light, fresh fruits, fresh and colorful flowers, fragrant incense, musical instruments, etc.** in order to create **merit** that is highly conducive for the nourishment of spiritual practice.
3. The lama's throne should be beautifully decorated, and this throne must be higher than the seat of the receiver of the Refuge ordination.

Preparation by the receiver of the Refuge ordination

The Refuge ordination receiver **must** view the lama as being the same as the living Buddha Shakyamuni. The lama may be in the form of an ordinary person but his ritual performances are not different from the Buddha's activities. It is not enough for you simply to think that the lama is like a Buddha. Rather view him **as** the Buddha. Keep this view during the entire ceremony.

First, the receiver of the Refuge ordination must make effort to bring his or her mind into an unbiased state free from normal clinging attachment to friends and loved ones and free from aversion towards those who cause harm and treat us badly. Sustain this **unbiased mind** for a few seconds before moving to the next step.

Second, understand that you are here to take the Refuge ordination through **your own choice** without being influenced by anyone else. A sense of joy must be generated in your mind and heart. Sustain this **joy** in your heart for a second before moving to the next step.

Third, make yourself see or think of the reason why you chose to take Refuge. You take Refuge in order to attain enlightenment for the benefit of all living beings that are constantly tormented by the pain and suffering whose root cause lies within them. Your **motivation** to take Refuge must evoke love and compassion towards all living beings that are like yourself in wanting happiness and not wanting even the slightest pain. Sustain the force of **love and compassion** in your heart for a few seconds without questioning before moving to the next step.

Fourth, your feeling of love and compassion induces a **strong wish** to help others to fulfill their fundamental aspiration to be happy and not to suffer. Sustain this strong wish for a second before moving to the next step.

Fifth, hold this strong wish—supported by the force of love and compassion—to release all living beings from the ocean of samsara by means of attaining enlightenment. While holding this wish, you are required to make **three prostrations** to the image of the Buddha while imagining that the real living Buddha is present to witness your intention.

Throughout the Refuge ceremony, you **must remain focused** in holding these thoughts:

The reason why you are taking Refuge
The function of the Refuge
A feeling of love and compassion
The strong wish to help others
Seriousness for attaining enlightenment no matter how long it takes and how painful the work might be
Unquestioning trust in the guidance of Buddha

Ceremonial activities to be performed by the lama or preceptor at the beginning

First, the lama invites the Buddhas and Bodhisattvas from the ten directions to be present in the room and to preside over the ceremony and witness your intention in taking Refuge.

Second, the lama makes heartfelt offerings as a token of pure intention, and to delight the enlightened mind.

Third, the lama deeply imagines that the Buddhas and Bodhisattvas delightfully accept the offerings and that this acceptance creates merit and purifies the delusive and cognitive obstructions.

Activities of the receiver of Refuge ordination

1. While viewing the lama as the living Buddha you should engage in the **mandala offering** as a token of your earnest desire and request to take Refuge ordination.

The Mandala Offering:

Sa Shee Po kyi Juk Shing May Tok Tram!
Ree Rab Ling Shee Nyee Da Gyen Pa Dee!
Sang Gey Shing La Mik Tey Bul War Yee!
Dro Kun Nam Dak Shing la Cho Pur Sahug!!

Jey tsun lama Dam Pa kyeh Nam kyee!
Cho kuy Kha la Kyen Tse Chu Zin trig!
Jee Tar Tsam Pay Dhul Jey Zin ma La!
Zab Gyeh Cho Kyee Char Pa Aob Tu Sol!!

IDAM GURU RAT NA MANDAL LAKAM NIR YA TA YA MII!!!

2. You next make your **sincere request** to the lama to give the Refuge ordination from your humble and respectful heart by reciting:

From today until I [you are required to say your name here] attain enlightenment for the sake of all living beings, I shall never give up my altruistic intention and effort under any circumstances whatsoever.

In order to ingrain this intention in my heart, May I be granted the Refuge ordination so that I may seek the guidance and support from the Three Jewels—Buddha, Dharma, and Sangha.

Repeat this request three (3) times from the depths of your heart. At the end of the third repetition, you are required to imagine that the lama has accepted your request through seeing or sensing your sincere intention. Remain with this feeling for a few seconds before moving to the next step.

3. Here you are required to **stand up** from your seat and make three prostrations to the lama or preceptor. After the prostrations, you must sit as shown in the illustration. Slightly bend your head down by pulling your chin towards the chest and then remain focused.

4. While maintaining this position, repeat the **Refuge formula** (Sanskrit, Tibetan and English versions) three (3) times together with the lama:

Na mo Guru Bhey!
Na mo Buddha Yah!
Na mo Dharma Yah!
Na mo Sangha Yah!!

Lama la Kyab su chi Wo!
Sangey la Kyab Su Chi Wo!
Cho La Kyab Su Chi Wo!
Phak pay Gendun Nam La Kyab Su Chi Wo!!

I go for Refuge in the Buddha,
The teacher of supreme
Truth and the unfailing guide.

I Go for Refuge in the Dharma,
The peaceful path consisting
Of love, compassion, ethics, and wisdom.

I go for Refuge in the Sangha,
The true source of
Inspiration and courage to walk on the path to
Enlightenment.

5. Right after the end of the third repetition, the lama will make **finger snap** to confirm that you have received full Refuge ordination. You must imagine that you have received it with a sense of joy and accomplishment in your open and exposed heart. Remain with this feeling for a few seconds. From today on, you are fearless in declaring yourself a Buddhist in the face of truth.
6. Now, with a sense of joy you may take your seat to receive your Refuge name.
7. You receive your **Refuge name** from the lama along with a white silk scarf, to be a sacred object of remembrance and which must never be forgotten for the rest of your life.

Your Refuge name will be related to the Dharma and the outstanding Dharmic qualities which can be attained only through Dharma practice. For example, if your Refuge name is **Sherab Gyatso**—which means the Ocean of Wisdom—through Dharma practice you need to be especially eager to acquire the Ocean of Wisdom in yourself rather than simply keeping your Refuge name card in your wallet or purse.

Conclusion

The Lama will do the final conclusion with dedication and auspicious prayers.

Appendix

FOOD BLESSING PRAYER

This is the food blessing prayer through which you offer the first portion of the food or drink that you consume.

> *Ton Pa Lamey Sangey Rinpoche*
> To the precious Buddha, you who show the unfailing path;
> *Kyob Pa Lamey Dam Cho Rinpoche*
> To the precious Dharma, one that protects from all seen and unseen miseries;
> *Dren Pa Lamey Gendun Rinpoche*
> To the precious Sangha, the ultimate source of inspiration
> *Kyab Ney Kon chok Sum La Cho Pa Bhul!!*
> I humbly offer (the essence of this food or drink) to the Three Precious Jewels.
>
> *Kha zey Myen Dang Dra war Rig pa Ye*
> With an understanding that food is like a medicine,
> *Do Chak Shey Dang may Per Tyen Gyi Tey*
> I eat it without hostility or attachment.
> *Gyak Chir Ma Lak Nyem Pay Chir Ma Lak*
> Not for haughtiness, might,
> *Tsak Chir Ma Lak Lu Ney Bha Shik Chi!!*
> Or robustness, but solely to sustain my body.

Here you should deeply imagine that the food or drink is being blessed by the Three Jewels and that thereby it turns into nectar or ambrosia to nourish your body so that you have strong and good health enabling you to engage in the Dharma practice and to work for the well-being of living beings. Then recite:

> *Dak Sok khor Chey Tse Rab Tham Chey Duh*
> In all rebirths, myself and all others:
> *Kon Chok Sum Dang Nam Yang Mey Drel Shing*
> May we never be apart from the Three Jewels,
> *Kon Chok Sum Po Gyun Du Cho pa La*
> And may we always be able to make excellent offerings to the Three Jewels.
> *Kon Chok Sum Gye Jin Lab Jug Par Shaug!!*
> May the blessings of the Three Jewels enter into us in all time and space.

* * *

PROSTRATION MANTRA

This is the prostration mantra to be recited when you perform prostration.

> *Kon Chok Sum La Chak Tsel Lo!*
>> I bow and prostrate to the Thee Jewels.

> *Om Namo Manjushri Ye!*
> *Namo Su Shriye!*
> *Namo Utamma Shriye So Ha!!*

You can also choose any of the following mantras when you perform prostration based on your personal needs and predisposition.

> ****Teya Tha! Om Muni Muni Maha Muni Yeh So Ha!!*

> ****Om Vajra Sattva Hung Phed!!*

> ****Om Bhen Zah Guru Padma Siddhi Hung Phed!!*

> ****Om Mani Pad Mey Hung!!*

Whenever you perform prostration you should immediately make dedication by reciting the following prayer:

By the force of the merit and virtue that I have created
Through performing prostrations,
May it become a powerful cause to attain enlightenment
For the benefit of all living beings without exception.

May it be a cause for the Dharma to prevail in all directions.
May it be a cause for enlightened beings and Lamas to live long.
May it be a cause for Bodhisattvas' wishes and prayers to be fulfilled.
May it be a cause for the entire earth to be covered with peace and happiness.

About the Author

"Geshe-la obviously has all the Buddhist knowledge and personal experience, and he reflects that with his calmness but also with an incredible sense of humor. He uses his amazing vocabulary to express complex concepts according to everyone's individual mental activity."

– **Charleston Magazine**

Geshe Dakpa Topgyal, a Tibetan Buddhist monk, was born in the Western region of Tibet, and fled to India at the age of six with his family due to the Chinese invasion of Tibet. He entered Drepung Loseling Monastery at the age of ten and received his Geshe degree (Doctorate of Religion and Philosoophy) twenty-two years later in 1992. Before coming to the United States, he taught in Europe for several years. He has been resident monk of the Charleston Tibetan Society in Charleston, South Carolina since 1996. He has written several Buddhist practice books.

Made in the USA
Charleston, SC
06 July 2011